More Fire!

The Building of *The Towering Inferno:*
A 50th Anniversary Explosion

by

NAT SEGALOFF

Author of
The Exorcist Legacy: 50 Years of Fear

More Fire! The Building of *The Towering Inferno*:
A 50th Anniversary Explosion
By Nat Segaloff
Copyright © 2023 Nat Segaloff
Second Edition

Published in the USA by:
BearManor Media, LLC.
1317 Edgewater Dr #110
Orlando, FL 32804
www.bearmanormedia.com

Perfect ISBN 979-8-88771-060-0
Case ISBN 979-8-88771-061-7

BearManor Media, Orlando, Florida
Printed in the United States of America
Book design by Robbie Adkins, www.adkinsconsult.com

More Fire!
The Building of *The Towering Inferno:*
A 50th Anniversary Explosion

by

NAT SEGALOFF

For David "Nebraska" Forbes and Stirling Silliphant
the two greatest gifts I got from
The Towering Inferno
And to firefighters everywhere

Table of Contents

Introduction: I Like to Watch

According to Mel Brooks, who is never wrong about such things, the difference between comedy and tragedy is, "comedy is if you fall down an open manhole and tragedy is if I get a hang-nail." Maybe this is why we love disaster films. The world can be ending, but as long as it's happening to someone else, we want to see them do the brodie down the manhole. Disaster films are a kind of mass rubbernecking in the way cars slow down to gawk at a roadside accident, invariably tying up traffic behind them (and often causing more accidents) just so they can cluck their tongues and say, "thank God it's not me." It's that mixture of morbid curiosity tinged with sadism and arrogance that carries over to the movies and has made the disaster film a genre unto itself.

The unspoken question asked by such films is why we take pleasure in other people's misfortune. Are we innocents like Chance the Gardener ("I like to watch") in Jerzy Kosinski's *Being There*? Or are we secretly itching to see what it looks like for a person to be stung to death by killer bees in *The Swarm* (1978)? We're told to stand under a doorframe in case of an earthquake, but the movie *Earthquake* (1974) shows us that nothing we do is going to keep us from being crushed into tartare.[1] We knew that no one really drowned when the 1997 screen *Titanic* went down with 1,517 souls (especially the guy who ricocheted off the propeller), but we felt for them anyway and didn't avert our eyes. The reason is simple and it defines the essence of motion pictures: movies are a voyeuristic experience. Nothing exploits this more than disaster films.

Call it schadenfreude.

---

1 By the way, the Centers for Disease Control say never to stand under a doorframe; a table is safer.

Best of all, unlike passing an auto accident on a back road, nobody sitting safely in the audience has to actually rush in to perform a rescue; after all, it's only a movie. The bigger the danger, the less the obligation to intervene. One might be expected to help the victims of fire, flood, or crime. But what about tidal waves, earthquakes, planetary collisions, alien invasions, or bug-eyed monsters? The disaster has to be something that people can relate to.

Most folks have been stung by bees. Some have had close calls under water. Covid has raised consciousness about plagues. And we've all been burned. Thus when we see some-one in flames in *The Towering Inferno*, we know what it feels like at a very basic level and our imaginations can extrapolate the pain to imagine what the victim is going through, even if it's happening to a trained, protected stunt performer who has been set aflame for the amusement of the audience. The ability to relate to fire—to know how to use it as well as to fear it—is why *The Towering Inferno* stands alone. Even though we know we're watching a movie, we know how hard it is to control fire, even for the experts. The brilliance of the film is that the audience is constantly aware that, while making it, somebody could've really been hurt.

Perhaps the most astute explanation of its power comes from the man who exploited the genre better than anyone else and is the spirit behind this book: Irwin Allen. "I have a private theory," he shared in an un-aired 1977 public relations interview while he was getting set to produce *The Swarm* (1978). "I think we're all really Walter Mittys. We stand in front of the mirror in the morning and we conjure up some great experience we're going to have on that particular day, and we go out and face the world attempting to be heroes. Because the truth is, we'd all like to be heroes. When you couple that with what I think is the basic problem with human nature, I think something is missing in our individual ids and I think, strangely enough, and unhappily, we all like to attend accidents. You've never seen an automobile crash that didn't have fifty or sixty people around it. You never saw a fire engine racing through the streets that wasn't followed by a crowd of kids and some grownups. And when they finally reached the fire, one of the greatest difficulties is to hold back the fire line. The combination of wanting to be the heroic Walter Mitty character and the fact that we enjoy accidents makes the present disaster movies the hits that they are. It gives the Walter Mittys of the world the opportunity to vicariously enjoy the thrill of being a hero while watching a terrible disaster in which they can't be hurt from the comfort of the theatre seat. The problem with our individual ids is that we're all madly attracted to disaster. And I think those two, more than anything else, plus the way you put it on the screen, result in the success of the disaster film—and for which I'm terribly grateful."[2]

The Towering Inferno wasn't the first disaster film, nor was it the last, but it was the biggest and the best. It took the financial resources of two Hollywood studios to get it made, and it was the crowing achievement of its fifty-eight-year-old producer who could not have known at the time that his career had hit its zenith and that everything he did afterwards would be downhill. Allen's story and the history of his greatest film cannot be told separately. Like the fictional 138-story skyscraper[3] which was built with a fatal defect, so, too, was Irwin Allen.

He was a tireless self-promoter who garnered so much success early in his career that the self-promoting was justified. In an industry that ran on smoke and mirrors, he was flesh and blood (and fire). He had confidence born of actual achievement, not presumed expertise. Although he and modesty were strangers, he was often quick to acknowledge the work of those around him. As a producer he provided everything his cast and crew needed, and he was near-maniacal about safety on his hazardous productions. He was vain but charming about it, and at heart was a sentimentalist about the movie business that he so dearly loved. If he had flaws, they were the flaws of passion.

---

2 Special features on 2003 DVD *The Towering Inferno*

3 At this writing the Burj Khalifa in Dubai, United Arab Emirates is the world's tallest building at 2,717 feet, or more than half a mile and 162 floors.

And yet, despite his flaws, Irwin Allen saved my life, even though he never knew it. While his film was still shooting in the summer of 1974, I was hired by a marketing visionary named David M. Forbes who had been handed the mandate by Twentieth Century-Fox[4] to assemble a special publicity unit that would make *The Towering Inferno* known nationwide. The team would supplement the work of the studio's own superb ad-pub department headed by Jonas Rosenfield, Johnny Friedkin, and Ashley Boone. At the time, I was publicity director for Sack Theatres, Boston's leading intown theatre chain. Having worked with many of the film company publicists whose releases played in our theatres, whatever PR skills I possessed were known to them and, when David asked around about who could take charge of *Inferno*'s northeast publicity, my name came up. He hired me, I joined the Publicists Guild (where I am a member in honorable withdrawal status), and David and I began a friendship which endures to this day. Not until years later did I learn that David had been warned not to hire me because Sack Theatres might seek revenge with a boycott of Fox product. Fortunately, *The Towering Inferno* and another Fox film released at the same time, Mel Brooks' *Young Frankenstein*, were such inescapable hits that no boycott ever took place if, indeed, the threat was real. I never forgot David's loyalty, and I also never forgot Irwin Allen, albeit for vastly different reasons, as you will soon read.

If my feelings about him, at times, seem mixed, they are. Like Allen, I love the movies but, unlike Allen, I believe it's incumbent on those who make movies to preserve the history of how they were made. Apparently Allen saved nearly everything about his films and almost nothing about himself. Given his ego, this decision is unfathomable. What could he possibly have been ashamed of? How can one understand his films without understanding the man? All I can do is speculate, and that's what I have done throughout this book where there was no other road to take. I appreciate those who spoke with me on and off the

---

4 At the time, Twentieth Century-Fox was hyphenated.

record and regret those who, for whatever reason, would not. It isn't like I was writing about the Manhattan Project.

This book is not just about the making of *The Towering Inferno*. It is also about the making of Irwin Allen, the mystery of his life, and his legacy as a filmmaker. It is a look at the effect the movie had on the public and the social milieu into which it was released. It is also about the fascination of fire, which the film exploited and which remains a (dare I say?) burning issue in the building trade.

Irwin Allen was a showman for half a century. Fifty years is a remarkable span on the Hollywood timeline in a town when careers can come and go in less than a decade, and sometimes with a single movie. Fortunately, the Margaret Herrick Library of the Academy of Motion Picture Arts and Sciences preserves the past; their voluminous records have saved the deadlines of more writers than can be counted, including this one. I want to thank their Director, Matt Severson; Chief Acquisitions Archivist Howard Prouty; Senior Research and Special Projects Librarian Elizabeth Youle; Senior Reference Librarian Genevieve Maxwell; and the other dedicated Herrick staffers for all that they do, have done, and will do for motion picture history and the scholars who chronicle it.

I also want to thank, for assorted reasons (some of them best left unsaid), those who, over the years, have enriched my knowledge of the film industry in general and *The Towering Inferno* in particular. They are, alphabetically, Carole Aaron, Andrew Abbott, George and Pauline Abdon, Gordon Armstrong, Ashley Boone, Kevin Burns, Danny Downey (Stuntmen's Association of Motion Pictures), F. X. Feeney, Carl Ferrazza, A. Alan Friedberg, Johnny Friedkin, Hope Miller Goldsmith, Robert Gollnick, Nico Jacobellis, Steve Jaffe, Mark Kermode, Edgar Knudson, Barry Krost, Russell Leven, Mallory Lewis, Don Morgan, Scott Newman, Wallis Nicita, Beverly Noble, Hal Potter, George Raymo, Jonas Rosenfield, Nat Rudich, ScriptFly.com, Mac St. Johns, Hal Sherman, Teller, David Traister, Robert Vaughn, and Mark Zavala.

I marvel at the research done by Marc Cushman, Jeff Bond, and Mark Alfred who waded through the Irwin Allen papers maintained by Derek Thielges at Prometheus Pictures. These are the legacy of Kevin Burns and Sheila Mathews Allen and are an unequaled resource for scholars as well as fans. I underline my thanks to Marc Cushman.

Thanks also, plus my love, to Tiana (Mrs. Stirling) Silliphant and the Estate of Stirling Silliphant for permission to reprint interviews and material curated by the author. She, he, and I first met when I arranged their publicity schedule for *Inferno* back in 1974 and stayed in touch ever since, something that rarely happens in Hollywood, the happy result of which led to my being asked to write his posthumous biography (*The Fingers of God*, Bear-Manor Media, 2013).

Particular thanks to my agent, Lee Sobel, for his skill and, most of all, friendship, and to my friend Ben Ohmart whose BearManor Media is a resource for film and pop culture history, much of it told by the people (the authors) who lived it. I share his love of movies, especially the flammable ones.

Nat Segaloff
Los Angeles

Chapter 1: What is a Disaster Film

There was a time when the people who made disaster films defensively insisted on calling them "group jeopardy" movies. This was, no doubt, a ploy to keep *Variety* from using the term *disaster* against them in a negative review or box office report. But it was also a way of stressing the human elements over the special effects in these productions, even though it was the special effects which drew audiences into the theatres. To be sure, these movies had their flaws. If there is any criticism that is most frequently leveled against them it is that the members of the jeopardized group were not defined well enough to care about them.

The Towering Inferno is different, as will be shown.

Many people think a disaster picture is any film in which a small number of characters fall into danger from a cataclysmic event. This is a pretty broad definition, and it has relatable, real-world counterparts in the effects of present-day climate change, coronavirus, Ebola, pollution, water shortages, and other actual threats that affect every human being on earth. There are also manmade mass disasters such as cyberattacks, terrorism, economic disparity, and loss of habitat. For Hollywood's purposes, however, disasters are anything tangible and unstoppable, no matter what their cause, that affect a small group of individuals, preferably movie stars.

Said Ronald Neame, who directed Irwin Allen's 1972 disaster film, *The Poseidon Adventure*, "The moment you've got a group of people in jeopardy and you know enough about each of them to care a little bit about them, you are held. You are gripped."[5]

The key to Neame's remark lies in "you know enough about them."

---

5   Neame quote from *Fire in the Sky, Hell Under Water*, Nobles Gate, Ltd., 2003.

Robert Vaughn, who co-starred in *Inferno*, added, "I think people go to see disaster films, or any film, to get away from their own lives which are nasty, brutal, and short, as many philosophers have said."[6]

"There *are* disasters," said stunt performer Loren James, "there *are* earthquakes that do horrible damage. There *are* floods that happen. There *are* avalanches. There are all these things that really happen in real life, and I think maybe that's something that gets people excited because it's something that could happen to them, and I think it makes it more personal and they get really caught up into it."[7]

There is another school of thought, a psychological one, explaining the success of disaster pictures as a way of defusing the stress caused by frightening, real-world issues. In that regard, the timing of history worked for both *Poseidon* and *Inferno*.

"We were coming off a difficult time in our country's history," opines David Forbes, who coordinated the marketing for *The Towering Inferno*. "Vietnam, all the protests and political activity, and then along came movies with great disasters—and also great heroes."[8]

The choice of threat is important. Any old disaster just won't do. It cannot be mundane. It must be pervasive and indiscriminate, if not Apocalyptic, something that could be on the cover of a book of worst case scenarios. It also has to be cinematic (plagues are hard to film, although it's been done.) For example, an action drama about a B-17 bomber crew on a mission over Germany in World War II may technically be a group jeopardy film, but it's not a disaster film because the crew knew what they were getting into and has the means to deal with it. Neither is a horror movie about a bunch of kids braving it out in a haunted house because they're the only ones in danger. A bona fide disaster movie is one in which the Four Horsemen are waiting in

---

6   Vaughn quote from *Fire in the Sky, Hell Under Water*, Nobles Gate, Ltd., 2003.

7   James quote from *Fire in the Sky, Hell Under Water*, Nobles Gate, Ltd., 2003.

8   Interviewed in *Hell Under Water, Fire in the Sky*, Nobles Gate, Ltd., director Andrew Abbott, 2003.

the wings. And it needs a little something "extra": the audience must identify not only with the people but with the threat.

Airport (1970) fits this definition. One of the first in the modern cycle of disaster pictures, it concerns a suicide bomber who blows a hole in a Boeing 707 during an international flight and both the crew and the airport must prevent tragedy. The stakes are raised by having the airport socked in by a snowstorm, an overworked manager heading for divorce, a captain having an affair, and his inamorata announcing that she is pregnant. In this case the triggering event is caused by a human, but the group is nonetheless in jeopardy. Notably, despite a full passenger manifest, only a handful of characters are well-defined, including Helen Hayes, who won an Oscar® for her role. Surely the effectiveness of *Airport* is grounded in the public's pervasive fear of flying, as numerous sequels and spoofs have proved. And yet—and this is a construction problem that plagues most disaster films—the actual disaster doesn't happen until nearly the end of the movie. The build-up is character development, something modern filmmakers don't mind abbreviating. When producer Irwin Allen and screenwriter Stirling Silliphant embarked on both *The Poseidon Adventure* and *The Towering Inferno*, they realized this shortcoming and crafted those films to get down to business as quickly as possible, letting the characters define themselves as they faced the danger. It was a lesson that has been heeded by successful disaster filmmakers ever since.

As with *Airport*, the most effective disaster movies involve something with which the audience is familiar and, if possible, already nervous about, if not downright frightened. The threat must be deadly and inescapable. These include Nature's revolt (volcano, earthquake, flood, avalanche, fire, creatures) human miscalculation (computers, war, Armageddon) and biological crossovers (plague, mutations). Sometimes they go from the sublime to the ridiculous such as with the nuclear monster movies of the 1950s such as *Them* (giant ants), *Tarantula* (giant spiders), *The Beginning of the End* (giant grasshoppers), and *Night of the Lepus* (giant bunny rabbits. Honest).

The Towering Inferno is the love-child of Man and Nature. The fire that destroys the world's tallest building didn't come from anything as arbitrary as a lightning strike, it came from a relentless combination of the contractor's venality, a businessman's corruption, and the arrogance of those who thought they had their bases covered. But it was still a disaster film in the sense that fire—an uncontrolled force of Nature—puts a group of people in mortal danger. In line with that, the elements that go into group jeopardy films are straightforward: God, an act of hubris, or some monumental screw-up triggers the situation. The victims–make that potential victims, because everybody's life has to be in danger (no super-heroes allowed)—must be an assortment of types, preferably reflecting the demographic make-up of the viewing audience. Most of them are couples who need to resolve problems with their relationship. The duets also give each of them someone to talk to for narrative purposes. They must be strongly etched characters in conflict with each other who are forced to put their differences aside to face a common threat. Traditionally, several of them will die along the way, one of them will show cowardice while another shows bravery, and a select few will survive to tell the tale. Finally, the resolution—which is not necessarily a happy one—can be a warning to Mankind-at-large that this sort of thing could happen for real. It is often accompanied by a religious epiphany. (Who says Cecil B. DeMille had the patent on Biblical films?)

"The main reason *Towering* does work," wrote Gerardo Valero in 2014 commenting on a CGI-heavy renaissance of group jeopardy films, "is that, unlike the entries in the recent revival of the genre, the characters are well-defined and played with utter conviction, allowing the audience to feel some concern about who will make it out alive and who won't…it's easy to think back and remember what each of them was about." This is in contrast, he notes, with *Independence Day* (2012) and the 2005 *Poseidon Adventure* remake, "where I can recall there being three dark-haired women among the escapees and good luck telling each one from the others."[9]

---

9 Gerardo Valero, "An Appreciation of the Disaster Movie on the 40th Anniversary of *The Towering Inferno*," May 14, 2014, www.rogerebert.com. Having said this,

Memorable characters go a long way toward making a disaster film realistic, believable, and serious enough to feel threatening (although *Don't Look Up*, 2021, was a loving send-up of the genre). It's all a matter of degree; a flooded basement is an irritation but a tsunami is exciting, at least on film. An overturned canoe is annoying, but an overturned ocean liner is phenomenal. A speeding stagecoach is thrilling but an unstoppable bus is positively explosive. And a house fire is a tragedy, but a skyscraper fire becomes a blockbuster.

Thus fire, and thus *The Towering Inferno*.

Even though Man has tamed fire, he is still enough of an animal to fear it down to his very genes. Anyone who doubts the mounting anxiety that fuels *Inferno* need only recall the monstrous images of people jumping to their deaths from the 104-story World Trade Centers on September 11, 2001 to avoid being burned alive.

In their nearly 130-year history, the movies have been no stranger to fire. One might even say that the movies were born in flame. Silent filmmakers looking for gripping subject matter readily dispatched camera crews to capture footage of local fires, then shot new footage to create a framing story around them.

Barring new discoveries, the first American fictional storytelling film was "The Life of An American Fireman" produced in 1902 by the Thomas A. Edison Company and released in January 1903. Directed by Edison's workhorse technician, Edwin S. Porter, the short runs six minutes and fifty seconds at sixteen frames per second as restored by the Paper Project of the Library of Congress. It shows a fireman dreaming of a mother and child, somebody pulling a fire alarm box (reportedly one of the screen's first close-ups), horse-drawn fire units racing to quell the fire, and a firefighter's rescue of a mother and child (presumably those in the dream) from the burning second story. Inspired by, but not fully understanding, the way French filmmaker Georges Méliès

---

Valero then complains that the script is too detailed, "conveying every single angle of its numerous characters and their individual stories."

had been making storytelling films since at least 1902's "A Trip to the Moon," Porter didn't actually plan "Fireman" as a narrative. He cobbled together several earlier Edison "views" that had already run in peep show parlors. These included assorted shots of fire brigades (there are four separate ones shown in the film though they are presented as a single responding company), staged interior scenes of a second-floor apartment fire (notably with smoke and no flames), the alarm being pulled, and a clever double exposure combining the dreaming fireman with the mother and child. No attempt is made at smooth cutting between shots; the same firemen seen sliding down the pole from the firehouse's second story at one angle are shown again doing the same thing from street level, and the rescue of the mother and child is shown first from inside and then repeated as they are being carried down the exterior ladder.[10] Over the years, attempts were made to re-edit "Fireman" to anticipate cross-cutting, but these were done after-the-fact. Nevertheless, the subject matter of fire is an emblem of an America when homes were still largely built of wood, and audiences knew it.

"The Life of an American Fireman" was so successful that Porter was inspired to make another storytelling film later in 1903, this time starting from scratch with a script. With the caveat that it was planned from the git-go, as opposed to being assembled after the event, "The Great Train Robbery" is rightly considered the first true American narrative film.

It has been discovered, however, that "The Life of an American Fireman" was in all probability influenced by a British film the previous year called "Fire!" Made by James Williamson for his Williamson Kinetograph Company and released in England on October 15, 1901, "Fire!" pulls no punches. A British bobby spots a fire in a row house and summons the local fire department who race to the scene. As Porter would do a year later, the firemen rescue victims from a burning room which, unlike "Fireman," is

---

10 Sharp-eyed viewers will also spot a framed logo for the Thomas A. Edison Company on the wall of the burning room, a device used by the ever-vigilant Edison to protect his copyright in the years before the U.S. Copyright Office had provisions for registering motion pictures.

actually in flames. Williamson reportedly shot his four minute, forty-seven second film at the abandoned Ivy Lodge in the seashore town of Hove, setting it on fire for the camera.[11]

It's tempting to draw a line from "Fire!" and "The Life of an American Fireman" to *The Towering Inferno*, which was made more than seventy years later. All of them ask their audiences to face one of Mankind's primal fears through identification with screen characters in jeopardy of being burned to death. Although, as we will learn, Allen used real fire because there was no way of faking it effectively on screen, the movies have a history of honest fakery in service of entertainment. As they grew up, so did the technique of making them.

Effects photography evolved gradually but consistently over the decades with the development of faster film stocks, better lighting, and craftspeople stretching to meet creative challenges. Pioneers such as Méliès, Willis O'Brien, Linwood Dunn, Eustace Lycett, Eugen Schüfftan, Stanley Horsely, Farciot Edouart, Albert Whitlock, Ub Iwerks, and Ray Harryhausen, among other wizards, broke ground for modern special effects masters like Douglas Trumbull, Richard Edlund, John Dykstra, Dennis Muren, Gene Warre, Jr. and a whole new sub-industry which today dominates mega-budget filmmaking. All of them work with one common goal: to make fantasy look real. Their room-sized rendering banks of computers and scores of digital artists are a huge change from the days when model animator Ray Harryhausen worked alone moving dinosaurs a quarter inch at a time on a tabletop set with a Dynamation® projector flashing previously shot backgrounds frame by frame behind it.

Even when the appropriately named Academy of Motion Picture Arts and Sciences was formed in 1927 it took them three years to begin conferring Scientific and Technical Awards, by which time only those early practitioners who were still working would be eligible to receive them.[12]

---

11 http://www.screenonline.org.uk/film/id/520632/index.html

12 Oscars, Gordon Sawyer Award, and other honors were given to Willis O'Brien (1950); Ray Harryhausen (1991); Ub Iwerks (1959, 1963, 1964); Linwood Dunn (1944, 1978, 1980, 1984); Albert Whitlock (1974, 1975); Farciot Edouart (1937, 1938, 1939,

For decades, movie magic was "practical," that is, the ingenious use of physical devices to produce effects that would look real on the screen. Papier mâché boulders, chocolate syrup blood (for black and white movies), sugar glassware and balsawood furniture that shattered on impact, miniatures, sets built in forced perspective, and mattes (scenery and buildings painted on glass suspended in front of the camera) were in common use. German cameraman Eugen Schüfftan invented an eponymous process that involved a matte painting with a mirror angled to catch view of an actor, thereby combining, for example, a real doorway with a huge painted castle. Rear projection and, later, blue screen processes were developed to allow actors to be photographed in a studio against a background that had been shot separately. Bit by bit the technology advanced and, with it, the filmmakers' freedom to imagine.

A crucial creative demarcation arrived in 1985 when computer generated images were integrated into a live action film in *Young Sherlock Holmes*. For a sequence in which the hero fights a two-dimensional knight who leaps from a stained glass window, the special visual effects innovators at George Lucas's Industrial Light and Magic devised a way to marry photorealistic animation with photographic reality.

Special visual effects, of course, are as old as the movies. What they could never manage to do until CGI, however, was make miniaturized fire and water look real. Even shooting flames and waves in slow motion wasn't completely convincing. The physical characteristics of fire and water are such that, when they are miniaturized and slowed down, they still look like, well, fire and water that have been miniaturized and slowed down. Even the parting of the Red Sea in both versions of Cecil B. DeMille's *The Ten Commandments* (1923 and 1956), despite brilliant optical printing and the use of 300,000-gallon dump tanks on the Paramount lot, cannot approach the digital reality of the water

---

1941, 1942, and two each in 1943, 1947, 1955); Eustace Lycett (1964, 1971). A notable lapse is Stanley Horsely whose work on *The Invisible Man* (1933) still baffles people. (Partial list)

in James Cameron's *The Abyss* (1989) and *Titanic* (1997), both of which, of course, used CGI.

It's hard to know which developed more quickly: filmmaking technology or the audience's ability to spot it. *The Towering Inferno* needed both fire and water to tell its story, and both had to look convincing despite 1974 filmmaking science standing in the way. How the production team overcame those challenges with ingenuity is what makes their achievement so astonishing and has kept the results memorable for half a century.

The rest of the miracle is how the film even came to be made at all. It involves more than Hollywood wheeling and dealing; it was the product of a love story between a man and the movies, and it begins on June 12, 1916 in New York City.

Chapter 1 Sidebar: The Burning Screen

Why does man find a flickering flame seductive and yet fearsome? Speaking to *LiveScience*'s Natalie Wolchover, Daniel Fessler, an evolutionary anthropologist at the University of California, Los Angeles, believes that an adult's fascination with fire is rooted in not having mastered it as a child. He reasons that humans have evolved ways of controlling fire, but because we no longer depend on starting it every day, we have lost our intimate relationship with flame and now relate to it in an abstract way.[13] (Except perhaps for cookouts.)

The movies likewise are drawn to fire and have devised ways of handling it, not only as an element in their stories but how to master it on the screen.

American movies have long since left "The Life of an American Fireman" in the nitrate dust but haven't really distanced themselves from its inspiration. In the hundred and twenty years since Edwin S. Porter chased fire engines into history, motion pictures have found thrills, suspense, life, death, and profits by setting things ablaze.

For over half a century even the film itself was flammable. From the first nitrocellulose photographic film developed by George Eastman[14] in 1889 to its replacement in 1952 by nonflammable cellulose acetate film stock, 35mm movies were volatile in every sense of the word. Cellulose nitrate as a clear base upon which to coat light-sensitive chemicals was first introduced as an advancement from cumbersome glass plate still photography. Pliable photographic film made

---

13   https://www.livescience.com/19853-fire-fascination.html

14   It was Reverend Hannibal Goodwin who devised a way to bond a pliable nitrocellulose base with photographic emulsion in 1887. The next year George Eastman purchased the patent rights from Goodwin and introduced the Kodak Brownie™ camera. In 1891 he began producing long strips of perforated film for Thomas Edison's motion picture camera. (Earl Theisen, "The History of Nitrocellulose as a Film Base," *Journal of the SMPTE*, Volume 20, March 1933.)

movies possible. There were, however, problems. Nitrocellulose is unstable and will start to break down chemically if stored above seventy degrees Fahrenheit and fifty percent humidity, which is pretty much the definition of everyday use. Even if stored in sealed cans, nitrate stock gives off gas which is prone to spontaneous combustion. When used under normal circumstances in the past, it was known to ignite while running through the projector. Worse, a nitrate fire is a chemical fire which defies all efforts to extinguish the flames; it even burns under water. This is why projection booths were sealed with glass panels to protect the audience if the film burned and the projectionist fled.

Nitrate fires were frighteningly common during the pre-1952 era. On July 6, 1937 a nitrate fire broke out in the Twentieth Century-Fox storage facility in Little Ferry, New Jersey resulting in two injuries, one death, and the destruction of most of Fox's pre-1932 library. On December 7, 1978 the National Archives at the Federal Center in Suitland, Maryland spontaneously combusted destroying thousands of titles made between 1929 and 1967. Even acetate titles stored there were destroyed, that's how hot the nitrate fire became. Today, remaining nitrate films are stored in climate controlled archival facilities such as New York's American Museum of Natural History, the George Eastman House in Rochester, New York, and other well-maintained locations. They can be screened only under tightly controlled conditions.

Non-flammable cellulose acetate stock was introduced in 1952. It had been available since 1923 for 16mm home movies but the image it rendered was deemed inferior for 35mm theatrical use.[15] Improved resolution emulsions for cellulose continued to dominate moviemaking until the photochemical process began being replaced by digital photography. The irony is that digital technology is so transitory (as any-

---

15 Katy Summerfield, "History of 16mm Film," *Artifact: A Southtree Blog,* undated. Additionally: Since the middle 1950s a more durable Mylar® base film has been used for release printing in 35mm and 16mm. It is less prone to burn in normal use.

one knows who has ever tried to open a DOS document in Word) that the only sure way to preserve our film heritage is by using the photochemical process. Film can last a hundred years if stored properly. Digital systems change so rapidly that a movie shot today might be rendered inaccessible in ten years. But that's another story.

As for the challenge of photographing fire itself, the conundrum was how to make flames look real on film (this will be addressed later) although it never stopped people from making movies about or with fire. When audiences saw real fire, they recognized it. They may not have been aware of the safeguards or tricks employed to keep it safe for those working with it (that was part of its power), but they knew it was real.

Because *The Towering Inferno* would not exist without the threat of fire, it might be illuminating to note earlier films that lit the fuse, so to speak. Chronologically, here are several in which fire plays a motivating or climactic role and the challenges faced by their filmmakers attempting to use it:

In Old Chicago (1937): Twentieth Century-Fox's Darryl F. Zanuck was trying to one-up MGM's Louis B. Mayer by making this epic of the 1871 Chicago fire to rival Mayer's earthquake drama, *San Francisco*. The Fox fire raged for four days on locations in Yuma, Arizona and Oakdale, California as the O'Leary brothers (Tyrone Power and Don Ameche) sparred over Alice Faye. And no, the fire was not started by Mrs. O'Leary's cow. It was also not started by H. Bruce Humberstone, a studio special effects man who bought trade ads taking credit, but was later revealed to have worked on scenes other than the fire.[16]

Gone with the Wind (1939): The burning of Atlanta remains one of the most thrilling sequences in all filmdom. It was shot on the back lot of the Selznick Studios (now

---

16 AFI Catalogue

the Culver Studios) in Culver City on December 10, 1938, the first official day of filming and long before a completed script had been written. The fire served two purposes: first, for the film, to tell the story of Union troops setting fire to the city but, secondly, for logistical reasons, clearing away old sets from the Selznick lot so Tara could be built. The "old sets" were the Temple of Jerusalem from Cecil B. DeMille's *King of Kings* and the three-hundred-foot tall great gate on Skull Island from *King Kong* (the shape of which is recognizable once one knows what it is). Selznick effects man Lee Zavits soaked the old timbers in oil, laid pipes that would deliver more oil, and then wired everything electrically to create sparks that would ignite the accelerants on cue. The Culver City Fire Department had only two trucks so Selznick called upon the Los Angeles Fire Department to stand by. Seven Technicolor cameras (all that existed at the time) covered it from various angles. Wide shots were captured upon which visual effects master Jack Cosgrove would add a silhouetted Rhett, Scarlett, the horse, and the wagon on the optical printer. For close shots, stunt performer Yakima Canutt (Rhett Butler was conveniently masked at this point in the story so no one could tell he was Canutt) led a horse and wagon with stunt performer Dorothy Fargo standing in for Scarlett O'Hara, who had not yet been cast. Melanie and the baby, of course, were out of view hiding in the wagon. According to legend (and confirmed by photos of guests invited to watch), agent Myron Selznick, David's brother, brought his client Vivien Leigh to the shooting and introduced her to the producer by saying, "David, I want you to meet your Scarlett O'Hara."[17]

The Ten Commandments (1956): Burning hail was one of the biblical plagues which the filmmakers solved using two techniques: the hail was popcorn dropped onto the floor of Pharaoh's palace from the rafters of the Paramount sound-

---

17   Ron Haver, *David O. Selznick's Hollywood*, New York: Alfred A. Knopf, 1980.

stage, and fire was real flames superimposed on that same floor. (Close inspection suggests that it might have been "ghost glass," that is, a time-proven theatrical trick of setting a huge pane of glass in front of the camera angled to reflect action in another part of the soundstage, in this case fire pots). The pillars of fire that stop Pharaoh's chariots as well as those that inscribe the ten commandments on Mt. Sinai were not, of course real fire but were obvious cartoons rendered by animator Joshua Meador who was borrowed by Paramount from the Walt Disney studio. In keeping with the then-current practice in the days of the old studio system, only department heads received screen credit, and thus it was Farciot Edouart and John P. Fulton whose names appear on the film despite thirty-one others doing the actual work under their command.[18]

Hellfighters (1968): John Wayne played Chance Buckman, a character based on Paul Neal "Red" Adair, a real-life expert at putting out oil well fires. The fire in the story was triggered by an unshielded light bulb that broke and sparked an immense oil blaze. Adair performed his specialty with explosives, water cannons, and bulldozers, followed by drilling mud and concrete to cap off the burning well. Shooting was mostly in Houston, Texas and Casper, Wyoming.[19] To make the fire effects work on film, special effects crew Fred Knoth, Whitey McMahon, Herman E. Townsley, and Whitey Krumm devised a two-ring hose nozzle, one of which shot out flames and the other of which shot out water and ink (because ink washes off more easily than oil). In addition to "Red" Adair, the film's technical advisers were "Boots" Hansen and "Coots" Matthews. In 1991 Adair came out of retirement at the request of then-President George H. W. Bush to go to the Middle east to put out the oil fires that Saddam

---

18 Kudos to the Internet Movie database (IMDb) for noting uncredited people here and elsewhere.
19 *Variety*, April 19, 1968.

Hussein's army had set as they vacated Kuwait. Adair was 76 at the time.

Carrie (1976): Based on Stephen King's first published novel in 1974, Carrie (Sissy Spacek) is a bullied girl who, when she hits puberty, develops telekinesis, a power that her Christianist mother believes comes from Satan and feared would emerge. The film's penultimate climax is the school's senior prom where Carrie is humiliated by her classmates (William Katt, Amy Irving, and John Travolta, et al) and wreaks unrestrained revenge by shutting the Bates High School doors and killing everybody in a burning gymnasium. A cautionary tale as well as a fantasy for any kid who was ever bullied, its effects were by Greg Auer and Glen Pepiot. Co-star William Katt told interviewer Sean O'Connell that the film was shot without scrupulous safeguards. "I remember being on set when they lit off the fire," he said, "because we were doing stuff out of sequence, right? I was already supposed to be lying on the ground, dead. So they lit the stage on fire, and the actual soundstage itself caught fire. And the [assistant director] was screaming for everybody to get out, and Brian [De Palma] was yelling for the camera department to keep rolling. I thought that that was pretty funny. All the decorations, everything, caught fire, and I don't believe that that was intentional."[20]

City on Fire (1979): An oil refinery explosion sets a whole city ablaze. This film solved the problem of making fire look real on the screen by using real fire and destroying several city blocks in Montreal at a cost of $400,000 as fire brigades stood by. Cliff Cully did the mattes and William Cruse also did visual effects. A team of others worked the fire: Thomas L. Fisher, Carol Lynn, Frank Varbel, Cliff Wenger, Jr. and Cliff Wenger, Jr.

---

20   Sean O'Connell, "The Real-Life Reason Why Carrie's Climax is So Terrifying," *Cinema Blend*, October 29, 2014.

Firestarter (1984): It would figure that a story about a little girl (Drew Barrymore) who can start fires with her mental powers would feature consummate fire effects. These were supervised by Special Effects Foreman Mike Edmonson, Special Effects Technician James Fredburg, and a crew of four other experts working with uncredited visual effects expert William Cruse. The fires in the film (based on Stephen King's 1980 novel) were all real. The fireballs that shot through the air flew on wires, and when people bounced into the air aflame they were actually set on fire and tossed about on trampolines. The fifteen-person stunt performers worked under Glenn Randall, Jr.

Always (1989): Steven Spielberg's remake of the Spencer Tracy-Van Johnson-Irene Dunne wartime romantic fantasy *A Guy Named Joe* changes the main character from a combat pilot in World War II to a firefighting pilot manning a PBY Catalina that scoops up water to dump on forest fires. The film uses two types of fires, both of them real. One is stock footage shot during the 1988 Yellowstone National Park disaster that destroyed sixty-three percent of the park's acreage. That is integrated with a set of fake trees designed by special effects supervisor Mike Wood and his crew to burn on cue.[21]

Backdraft (1991): As with *Always*, even into the digital age, director Ron Howard chose to give his firefighter drama the legitimacy and excitement of actual fire. He summoned the legacy of 98 years of filmmaking experience and experimentation. Because flames and smoke obscure actors' faces, Howard's effects supervisor Brian "Pyro" Adams and his fifteen-man (all men) team used a "white, haze-like effect" to give the impression of smoke-filled rooms. Cardboard ash floated around when needed, guided by blowers that

---

21 AFI catalogue

"directed" the feathery pieces.[22] Pyrotechnicians added diesel fuel to traditional propane to generate pitch-black smoke for long shots, and dumped chemicals on the fires to make the colors more film-friendly.[23] They also used slow-motion and reverse-motion to imbue the fires with personality. When it came time for the flames to race toward the camera as if to assault it, trails of glue and other flammable substances were laid down with the camera protected in a fireproof box. *Backdraft* did its job so well that it was nominated for a Best Visual Effects Oscar.® Fans say that it represented the ultimate screen portrayal of fire before the age of CGI.

22 *Los Angeles Times*, May 29, 1991 and *New York Times*, June 9, 1991.
23 *Variety*, May 29, 1991.

Chapter 2: The Master of Disaster

1916 was a lousy year to be born in New York City. A terrible polio epidemic was declared that will kill two thousand people and cripple thousands more. D.W. Griffith's exculpatory epic *Intolerance* opened. America was slowly being nudged into The Great War despite President Woodrow Wilson's election promise to keep the country out. In international news, German U-boats held sway over the North Atlantic, T.E. Lawrence was creating havoc against the Turks in Arabia, Einstein announced his general theory of relativity, and both Converse and Keds introduced their signature canvas shoes, soon to be called "sneakers." Perhaps best of all, Nathan's Famous Frankfurters debuted at Coney Island. The Yankees finished fourth that season (the Boston Red Sox finished first, so there) but the city was still its brash, unstoppable self, and so were the people in it—in the Bronx, in particular, where Irwin Allen was born on June 12, 1916.

Allen's death certificate lists his parents as Joseph Allen of Russia and Eva Davis of New York. The information is suspect.

The fourth son (after brothers Rubin, George, and Fred) of a typical struggling Eastern European immigrant family, as countless others have said who shared similar childhoods, "We didn't know we were poor because everybody was poor." Irwin Grinovit knew it and never forgot, spending the rest of his life hiding the tarnish of poverty and making sure nobody else ever learned about his early struggles. Indeed, for a man with an ego the size of all five of New York City's boroughs, and who hired clipping services to send him everything about him that appeared in print, there is nothing in the public record on Allen as a person, only as a filmmaker. Either he sidestepped interviewers' questions throughout his career or they never thought to ask them. Everything that he allowed to be released for publication, apparently from the earliest times, was carefully managed. A browse through twenty years of prepared studio biographies (press releases traditionally included in publicity kits sent to journalists) reveals endless reshufflings of the same bland summary of his early life. For example, this is from a June 10, 1959 PR sheet from Allied Artists:

> *Born in New York City on June 12, 1916. After the briefest spell at City College of New York, he shifted to Columbia University, majoring in journalism and advertising, and at the end of his third year came to Hollywood on a summer vacation. One look at the place did it; he decided to remain.*
>
> *He signed on as an editor of* Key Magazine, *then quickly shifted to radio advertising and exploitation, and before anyone knew it had his own program on station KMTR. It was* Hollywood Merry-Go-Round, *the Peter Potter show of its day, which he soon changed to a Hollywood news program. And at t he same time he was writing a Hollywood column for Atlas Feature Syndicate, which appeared in 73 papers throughout the country.*

And this from August 13, 1979:

> *Irwin Allen created the first celebrity panel show ever produced in the United States. Through the show's four-year history, more than 1000 film stars and Hollywood celebrities made their television debut on his* Hollywood Merry-Go-Round.
>
> *But Allen, whose reserve of energy is boundless, continued to add to his fields of operation. While juggling a radio show, a newspaper column, as well as the celebrity television show, he opened a literary agency representing writers and literary material for the motion picture industry.*

. . .and so forth, endlessly rewritten with no details and barely fact-checked. Inasmuch as Allen had to approve his published biography, it is perhaps not surprising that this vagueness might have grown from a skepticism of reporters gained while studying to become one. While at Columbia he also studied advertising, and the skill and instincts of the tub-thumper never left him.

But the paucity of detail likely also stemmed from defensiveness about what he perceived to be a shameful past. It didn't matter how many others in the 'hood were poor, Irwin Grinovit didn't want to be thought of as one of them. This reflects the drive of second generation Americans to assimilate into society by distancing themselves from their immigrant parents, the result of which became the mantra of Hollywood's founding moguls, "from Poland to polo in one generation."

Young Irwin was no wallflower. He ran long distance track, managed his school's baseball team, and worked as a barker at a carnival where he no doubt gained his lifelong love of circus—and huckstering. His interest in sports was fueled by reading coverage in the papers, particularly the *New York Daily News,* whose star columnist was Paul Gallico, later to write the novel *The Poseidon Adventure* that made Irwin a fill scale mogul.

Allen's college years would have been in 1933 and '34 when the Depression was smothering dreams of two generations. He attended Columbia University at night and availed himself of the subsidized courses at City College of New York during the day. In his sparse free time he wrote press releases for the jazz clubs on fifty-second street and in Greenwich Village.

In 1938, Irwin and his cousin Al Gail (his closest relative, with whom he would collaborate in various capacities throughout his career) decided to head for Los Angeles. It made sense. Hollywood was emerging from the Depression ahead of the rest of America and, without knowing it, was about to embark on what has been called its greatest year, 1939. Irwin and Cousin Al drove cross country and never looked back. Somewhere along the web of the nation's endless promising highways, Irwin Grinovit became Irwin Allen. He was twenty-two.

Not long after he declared for California citizenship, his parents died, first his father, then his mother. In none of his biographies is there so much as a mention of their first names.[24] His own official biography says he and Gail joined the staff of California's *Key Magazine,* a local visitors guide not unlike those found in hotel rooms.[25] Gail wrote for them and Allen sold ads, getting him out of the office and into meetings with the advertising end of the movie, radio, theatre, and nightclub companies. Never at a loss for words, he also wangled a job as announcer/host on the all-night shift at KMTR-AM 570. Adept at both talking and selling, in 1941 he began a fifteen-minute weeknightly show he called *Hollywood Merry-Go-Round* (either a nod to, or a steal from, political columnist Drew Pearson's syndicated newspaper column, "The Washington Merry-Go-Round"). Allen developed a style of standing at the studio microphone while leaning over a table and reading his script. He punctuated his delivery with faux telegraph sounds not unlike national broadcaster Walter Winchell. KMTR had connections to the *Los Angeles Evening Herald,* and soon the newly minted Irwin Allen was writing his own column, "On the Set," for the Hollywood Features Syndicate.

The Hollywood Merry-Go-Round (which may sometimes have been called *The Irwin Allen Show*) was a phenomenon in an age when radio both kept filmgoers home and inspired them to attend movie theatres. Over the course of eleven years he interviewed countless celebrities and behind-the-scenes people, enriching his contact list and focusing his ambitions toward actually making movies instead of just talking about them.

KMTR was sold in 1946 and the new owners renamed it KLAC. *The Hollywood Merry-Go-Round* continued there until 1952, with a short-lived television counterpart from 1949-1951 on KLAC-TV. As the saying goes, Irwin Allen had a face made for radio; he never found a way to make what he did visually interesting. Nevertheless, his access and exposure drew him to Atlas Features Syndicate where he wrote a newspaper column under the same title as his show.

––––––––––––––––––

24 New York refuses to provide birth certificates to outsiders.

25 Except *Key* didn't start publishing until 1940 according to their website, *Key Magazine* website, https://www.keymagazine.com/.

There is no record of Allen serving in World War II.

In 1944—again, according to his approved studio biographies—he opened his own literary agency to represent writers selling their film rights. The more modest truth was that he went to work for the Orsatti Agency under brothers Victor and Ernest Orsatti. Ernest Orsatti was already a revered name when he joined his brother Victor as a ten-percenter; he was a star athlete, first baseman and outfielder for the St. Louis Cardinals and brought them to two world series. In 1972 Allen would hire Ernest's son, Ernie, as stunt performer on *The Poseidon Adventure* (q.v.) and again in 1974 on *The Towering Inferno*. Allen joined the Orsattis in 1947 as head of their thriving radio department while he himself was still being seen and heard on television and radio.

The Orsattis represented actors and writers. This was like having the keys to a gold mine. At the time, all the studios maintained aggressive story departments and depended on publishers and agents to send them galleys (not-yet-published manuscripts) in search of a movie sale. Allen, in addition to his other work, took on the role as agent and began hawking the literary works of the Orsattis' clients including Fanny Hurst, P.G. Wodehouse, and Ben Hecht. Although Hecht already had a prolific screenwriting career (*Spellbound, Notorious, Kiss of Death* and, uncredited, *Duel in the Sun, Lifeboat,* and *Gone with the Wind*), it was for writing originals or adapting the works of others, not his books. For whatever reason, there is only one instance of Hecht being hired to adapt one of his own books: *Miracle in the Rain* (1956) long after Allen left the Orsattis.

Hecht may have been a tough sell, but Allen found success with another client, the ageing Rex Beach, from whom he personally licensed the film rights to Beach's 1946 novel *The World in His Arms*. Allen quickly sold it to the recently-formed Universal-International Pictures, who would film it in 1952. The sale encouraged Beach, who had long wanted to dabble in film, to let Allen represent him.[26] Thus inspired, Allen became an early

---

26 Beach's most famous, and most-filmed work (no fewer than seven times), was *The Spoilers*. Beach's film dreams ended when his wife died in 1947; two years

"packager" who brought together several elements of a nascent film, offering buyers a ready-made production recipe. His dealings with the studios gave him not only an education but important, top-level entrée to exactly the people to whom he would need to sell his own projects.

As the 1940s became the 1950s, however, Allen had competition. Everybody in Hollywood did. It was called television. Movie attendance, which had hit ninety million a week in the postwar years, dwindled as TV sets invaded America's living rooms. He managed to get a foothold in shaky RKO studios by setting up *It's Only Money* which was scripted by Melville Shavelson from a story by Leo Rosten. This gave the picture an interesting pedigree. Shavelson at the time was known as a comedy writer, having supplied gags for Bob Hope's radio show before moving (with Hope) into feature comedies such as Hope's *The Paleface*, 1948, and *Sorrowful Jones*, 1949. He also scripted *Always Leave Them Laughing*, 1949, for Milton Berle and *The Kid From Brooklyn*, 1946 for Danny Kaye. He would later blossom as a writer-director with *The Seven Little Foys* (1955) and *The Five Pennies* (1959).

For his part, Leo Rosten sold occasional stories and screenplays to Hollywood but was better known as a novelist, essayist, and chronicler of Jewish humor such as *The Education of H*Y*M*A*N K*A*P*L*A*N*. The combination of Rosten and Shavelson should have graced *It's Only Money* with success; on top of them, it featured Groucho Marx. Yet the picture was burdened with behind-the-scenes intrigues, none of which enlivened the screen proceedings.

The story of a bank teller (Frank Sinatra) pressured by the mob and helped by a wisecracking waiter (Groucho), the picture actually starred Howard Hughes's protégé Jane Russell. Sinatra was third-billed as his career had yet to spring back from his bobby-soxer days. There was good reason for this, and it had nothing to

---

later, he took his own life. *The World in His Arms* starred Gregory Peck in a plot (runaway princess hides out with a common man) reminiscent of *Roman Holiday* (1953), which also starred Peck.

do with a horse's head in anybody's bed, although it did involve a vendetta. In 1950 Louis B. Mayer, the head of MGM, bought Sinatra's contract from the agency MCA who had, in 1943, bought it from Tommy Dorsey and Dorsey's manager, Leonard Vannerson, after starring Sinatra with Gene Kelley in *On the Town* (1949).[27] For unexplained reasons, Mayer shared Sinatra's contract with Howard Hughes, who put him into *It's Only Money*. Sinatra's behavior during filming both projects was so coarse that Mayer and Hughes delayed release of both his films in an effort to kill his career.[28] During the wait, Hughes changed the title of *It's Only Money* to *Double Dynamite* (a smarmy reference to Jane Russell's bosom) and shelved it until the end of 1951. Although Allen was sidelined by studio politics during *Double Dynamite*, he cemented a friendship with Groucho Marx. He even managed to develop a cordial relationship with the mercurial Howard Hughes. Nevertheless, Allen received no producer credit even though it was his efforts that got the film made.

Allen fared better with his next project, *Where Danger Lives*, which, because of Hughes' postponement of *Double Dynamite*, was released first, even though it was produced second. Allen was billed as associate producer while Irving Cummings, Jr. received full producer credit. It was scripted by Charles Bennett from another Leo Rosten story, "A Rose for Julie," the title under which it was filmed. Bennett figures heavily in Allen's oeuvre.[29] He was a playwright whom Allen would later hire to write several features and TV episodes. *Where Danger Lives* starred Robert Mitchum, Claude Rains, and Faith Domergue (also a Hughes protégé), and was directed by John Farrow, Mia's future father. A thriller in which, for a change, a dark-haired femme fatale

---

27 Richard Setlowe, "Sinatra's Done It His way, For Better or Worse," *Variety*, November 5, 1992. Any suggestion of Lucca Brazzi comes from the imagination of Mario Puzo, although there have always been rumors about MCA's reputed mob connections.

28 Jeff Bond, *The Fantasy Worlds of Irwin Allen*, CA: Creature Features, 2019.

29 Nevertheless, Bennett is quoted by Cushman and Alfred in *Irwin Allen's Voyage to the Bottom of the Sea, Volume I* as hating Allen despite working with him on project after project. Apparently politics has nothing on Hollywood when it comes to strange bedfellows.

(Domergue) lures a doctor (Mitchum) into a web of murder, it was one of a succession of low-budget pictures to which RKO banished Mitchum following his 1948 marijuana bust, not realizing that the bust only burnished the actor's rebel image.

From its glowingly successful days in the 1930s and 40s (*Top Hat, King Kong, Citizen Kane*, etc.), by the 1950s RKO was on the ropes. Weakened when its acclaimed team of producer Adrian Scott and director Edward Dmytryk (*Crossfire*, 1947) was blacklisted, the studio and its vast chain of theatres were acquired by Howard Hughes in 1948, more as a place for making starlets than making movies. Seeing *Where Danger Lives* take shape under someone else's guidance, Allen chafed at losing control. Nevertheless, in 1952 he and Cummings *fils* made *A Girl in Every Port*.[30] Like *Double Dynamite*, it starred Groucho Marx and added William Bendix and Marie Wilson. *A Girl in Every Port* should have been called *A Horse in Every Port* because it was about two sailors who acquire a lame race horse only to discover that it has a twin that knows how to win races. Scripted by Chester Erskine (best known for *The Egg and I*, 1947) from Frederick Hazlitt Brennan's story "They Sell Sailors Elephants" and directed by Erskine, it marked Groucho's last starring movie role, after which he moved to television and began the quiz show *You Bet Your Life*.

Under Howard Hughes, RKO was always in play. When he tried to sell the studio in 1958 to a Chicago consortium rumored to have mob connections, several stockholders sued. That attempt (with a little nudge from the Department of Justice) forced the sale of RKO to producer-investor and founder of Metropolitan Theatres Sherrill Corwin.[31] This elevated Allen—by attrition, it seems—to becoming RKO's head of production. The position lasted only a few months, but it was just the opportunity he needed. With the studio in disarray, even if he was nominally running it, Allen gave himself the greenlight to make a movie his

30 No relation to Howard Hawks' 1928 silent film of the same title.
31 Thomas M. Pryor, "New RKO Board Seemed Named Soon; Corwin Hopes for Appointment Also of President Over the Week-End at Studio, *New York Times*, December 6, 1952.

own way. He optioned marine biologist Rachel Carson's bestselling 1950 book, *The Sea Around* us and proceeded to direct (without credit), and produce and write it (with credit). Released in June 1952, *The Sea Around Us* won the Best Feature Documentary Oscar® at the 1953 Academy Awards.® Allen and editor Doane Harrison (Billy Wilder's favorite editor) pored through some 300 miles of 16mm film to winnow it down to its sixty-two minute length, barely qualifying as a feature.

A blend of science and poetry, the book kindled wide public recognition of the water that covers two-thirds of the earth's surface. Fitting it all into one movie was a formidable task. "First we broke down the various categories contained in Miss Carson's book," Allen told UPI's venerable Vernon Scott.[32] "There were seventy-five categories of subject matter. Next we started writing letters to all kinds of people and places for the film. In all, we contacted exactly 2,341 persons. My secretary handled more than 6,000 letters." Explaining that the documentary was cut down from 1,662,362 feet of film, Allen proudly noted that, "if we had shot this film from scratch, it would have cost us four-and-a-half million dollars. We brought it in for a little over $200,000." Narrated by Don Forbes and Theodore van Eltz, the picture ends on a prescient note that water temperatures in the arctic are rising, presaging warnings of climate change that would make headlines decades later.

The film was not without controversy. Ms. Carson herself objected to Allen's assertion that global warming would one day make the oceans rise high enough to inundate coastal cities. She held that the rise would be negligible and demanded changes in the documentary. Allen countered that the changes she wanted would cost almost as much as making the film all over again, and he refused.

The film had another repercussion. Walt Disney, who had been distributing his films through RKO, including his *True-Life Adventures* short subjects, had wanted to expand to feature-length nature films but was continually rebuffed by the studio's decision

---

32 Vernon Scott, United Press International/*Los Angeles Daily News*, July 2, 1953.

makers. Seeing *The Sea Around Us* get made instead of his own nature features riled Disney to the point where he canceled his RKO distribution contract and, with his brother Roy and Irving Ludwig, founded Buena Vista Distribution Company, named after the street on which his Burbank studios were built.

By 1954 Allen could see Hughes's writing on RKO's walls. He finished his RKO commitment with the 3-D Technicolor action film *Dangerous Mission*, receiving full producer credit. He left the studio in mid-April but surprised everyone by returning there two weeks later to launch his own company, Windsor Productions, announcing a financing deal for two pictures in the style of *The Sea Around Us*.[33] Six months later, however, he announced a deal with Warner Bros. to make "an epic scale feature documentary" called *The Animal World* and moved Windsor Productions to the WB lot.[34]

To a generation too young to have seen the seminal *The Lost World* (1925) or *King Kong* (1933) on their initial release, *The Animal World* (1956) is the film that inspired a fascination with dinosaurs, movie or otherwise. Written and directed by Allen and co-produced by Allen and George E. Swink (thereafter Allen's post-production supervisor), *The Animal World* is a documentary overview of the earth's land creatures in dry counterpoint to the wet world of *The Sea Around Us*. Originally intending to depend on artist's drawings to represent the earth's dinosaur antecedents, he was persuaded by stop motion expert Ray Harryhausen to use animated creatures.

"Harryhausen's judgment proved accurate enough," writes movie dinosaur scholar Donald H. Glut, "since the bulk of *The Animal World*, consisting mostly of nature footage, has been nearly forgotten by today's audience—who seem to remember hardly more than the film's dinosaurs."[35] No doubt their memory is assisted by a trio of 3-D View Master® discs of Harryhausen's dioramas.

---

33 *Variety*, March 2, 1954.
34 *Hollywood Reporter*, September 2, 1954.
35 Donald H. Glut, *The Dinosaur Scrapbook*, Secaucus, New Jersey: Citadel Press, 1980.

Inspired in part by Charles R. Knight's illustrations and in consultation with Dr. Charles L. Camp from the University of California, Harryhausen worked with his mentor, Willis O'Brien (who had animated both *The Lost World* and *King Kong*), to create several stunning scenes of grazing, hatching, and fighting creatures. The twelve-minute sequence took seventy-three days to complete.[36] When the picture was previewed, however, audiences reacted negatively to the film's violence, not only in the animated sequences but more disturbingly in the authentic live action nature footage. Allen was forced to make cuts to get a seal from the Motion Picture Production Code. Despite its reputation and containing the final O'Brien-Harryhausen collaboration, *The Animal World* remained tangled legally until its home video release in 2010, the apparent result of Allen not having obtained proper clearance from some of the nature photographers he had hired.

Plugging his film to Don Ross of the *New York Herald-Tribune*, Allen had accepted that the animated dinosaurs he once had rejected were the selling point of his picture. Alluding to his last two live-actin films, he joked, "After being around Groucho, I was glad to get to dinosaurs. The dinosaurs aren't so hysterical." He said that, since nobody knows what the creatures sounded like, he and his sound technicians, figuring that they were reptiles, took the hiss of snakes and "multiplied it 1,000 times and mixed it with the roar of a bull elephant."

Having exhausted sea and land creatures, Allen next turned his attention to homo sapiens in *The Story of Mankind* (1957) based on Henrick Willem van Loon's 1921 book. Although van Loon's measure for inclusion in his sardonic chronicle was whether the person or event in question had changed Man's fate (no, not a reference to Malraux), Allen's criterion in casting was what famous faces he could hire for cameos. The film had nothing to do with the book, and it's a good thing that the author had died in 1944. Written by Allen and Bennett in the form of a trial between the Devil (Vincent Price) and the Spirit of

---

36 *Los Angeles Times*, June 19, 1956.

Man (Ronald Colman), it's a sequence of flashback sketches illustrating moments of great pith, promise, and sometimes disaster. Allen inveigled a cast that would rival that of fellow producer Mike Todd who had innovated cameo roles in his production of *Around the World in 80 Days* the year before. One never knew who would pop up as what historical figure: Hedy LaMarr, Agnes Morehead, Peter Lorre, Dennis Hopper, Edward Everett Horton, Francis X. Bushman, Virginia Mayo, and John Carradine are just a few. Allen also included the Marx Brothers—Groucho, Chico, and Harpo—but, to the everlasting ire of Marxians, didn't think to put them together in the same scene.

The most remarkable thing about *The Story of Mankind* wasn't even in the film. Like *The Animal World*, it was released by Warner Bros. but at a cost that exceeded its budget, meaning that Allen negotiated a better deal for himself than for the studio. This rankled the reigning Jack L. Warner to the point where he never made another deal with Allen as long as he lived.[37] Warner did, however, exact revenge, although it was Pyrrhic. After a sneak preview in the San Fernando Valley to gauge audience reaction at which J.L. himself was present, everyone deemed the picture too long (Allen had wanted as three-hour epic). When the suggestion of cuts was raised, Warner declared, "Oh, let's just put it out," effectively euthanizing it.[38] *The Story of Mankind* was also the last film of Ronald Colman and Chico Marx (but not Irwin Allen).

One of the oddities of the way Hollywood does business is that it is unusual for "business as usual" to be the usual business. While Allen had production deals at both RKO and Warner Bros., in 1959 he set up a deal at Columbia to produce *The Big Circus* but, by the time the film was ready for release, it had been picked up by Allied Artists, and just to make it even more confusing it had been filmed at MGM. Like a big kid (although

---

37 Cushman and Alfred, *Irwin Allen's Voyage to the Bottom of the Sea, Volume 1*, CA: Jacobs/Brown Press, 2018. Extrapolated reference. Allen would partially return to the Warner family with *The Towering Inferno*.

38 Charles Bennett quoted by Cushman and Alfred, op cit. The film's running time is 100 minutes.

he was forty-three at the time) Allen finally got to join the circus, even if his kindred spirit, Cecil B. DeMille, had gotten there first with *The Greatest Show on Earth* in 1952.

In Allen's spectacle, a somewhat less than stellar all-star cast enacts the story of a clever showman whose attempts to rescue a failing circus are sabotaged from within. Performers include Victor Mature, Red Buttons, Rhonda Fleming, Kathryn Grant, David Nelson, Gilbert Roland, and Vincent Price. Allen and Bennett were joined by Irving Wallace in writing the script from Allen's original story; it's a reminder that Allen was not just a packager but a creative force who, more times than not, brought his own vision to the screen, directing his films wherever possible but also having the wisdom to know when to let others take the helm.

But that wasn't exactly true. Allen desperately wanted to direct *The Big Circus*. It was his milieu, his love, his dream. But Allied Artists was not about to allow him to be the ringmaster, even under his own big top, for the simple fact that he was not a good director. Sure, he brought his films in on time and on budget, but there was nothing on the screen to distinguish them. Instead, Allied Artists hired the colorless but more experienced British director Joseph N. Newman (most famous for the sf picture *This Island Earth*, 1955). The result was a sprawling drama interspersed with thrills (some of which were undercut by bad process photography) that barely broke even.[39]

As would occur many times in his career, Allen was disappointed at being denied the megaphone. But becoming known as a producer was more important in a town where directors could be replaced like dinner napkins.

For his next film Allen would keep a firm grip on his baby; directing the picture would be part of the deal going in. Here is where he began his association with Twentieth Century-Fox, a relationship that would change the course of both. It was *The Lost World*, an ambitious adaptation of Sir Arthur Conan Doyle's 1912 fantasy novel about a prehistoric land surviving atop a high

---

39 $2.7 million rentals on a $2 million budget, per *Variety*, January 6, 1960.

Amazon plateau and the stalwart team of adventurers, led by Professor Challenger, to explore it. Allen put up $100,000 for the Doyle novel and brought it to Fox who was eager to have a follow-up to their 1959 hit adaptation of Jules Verne's *Journey to the Center of the Earth*. They even considered shooting it in big-screen 70mm Todd-AO developed by Mike Todd and American Optical. Instead, they opted for CinemaScope, a widescreen process which they owned. They also allowed Allen to use some of the old interior sets from *Journey to the Center of the Earth* that were still standing.

Allen hired Claude Rains to play Doyle's feisty Professor Challenger and sought Peter Ustinov, Trevor Howard, Victor Mature, and Gilbert Roland (who'd had a miniscule unbilled role in the 1925 silent version). Allen and Bennett used a free hand to adapt the Conan Doyle novel, adding (of course) a woman, Jill St. John, to the cast that eventually included Michael Rennie, David Hedison, Fernando Lamas, and Richard Haydn along with Rains. Perhaps frustrated by the expense, length of time, and attention accorded Willis O'Brien and Ray Harryhausen for *The Animal World*, Allen opted to use gussied-up monitor lizards in place of stop-motion models to play Conan Doyle's dinosaurs (so had *Journey to the Center of the Earth*). O'Brien was, however, hired by the production to create atmospheric production sketches.

With the box office success of *The Lost World*, Allen became part of the Fox family. It was, however, a dysfunctional family. The company's co-founder Darryl F. Zanuck had announced his resignation in 1956; production head Buddy Adler had died in 1957; company President Spyros Skouras had no idea whom to appoint to fill the creative positions; and, in search of a blockbuster to remind the world of the studio's prestige, they hit upon the idea of remaking their 1917 Theda Bara starrer, *Cleopatra*.

All of this activity filled Allen's business life, but what did he do when he left the studio? "My sort-of theory when I was doing the book," said author Jeff Bond (*The Fantasy Worlds of Irwin*

Allen[40]), "was that he didn't really have a big personal life. He did, but it was so related to his work. He had friendships with famous actors and people in the business and socialized with them, otherwise he would be one hundred percent occupied in making the TV shows and movies and wasn't known for taking tons of work home–he'd spend full evenings supposedly going through scripts and artwork and things and planning his shows. The one thing we got in the book that I thought was hilarious and very last minute was that he had something going on with Joan Crawford for a while to the extent that her kids called him Uncle Irwin. It was right after the show *Feud* was on and Kevin (Burns[41]) called me up and said, 'I've got letters from Joan Crawford to Irwin.' But again that sort of goes into his just being a star-fucker. He liked celebrities, he liked hanging out with celebrities and, if he was going to date somebody, it would be a celebrity. He did, I think, have a starlet thing while he was making movies; it's not like he was above womanizing. I think he would probably be the classic kind of sexist Hollywood producer but not really like a ladies' man. It wouldn't matter, if you were a high-powered Hollywood producer how good looking you were, and he was not great looking, he was bald until he got his wig."[42]

Irwin Allen, by this time, had fully synchronized his talents and his ambitions. Given the $10 million gross[43] of *The Lost World*, on a budget of $1.515 million,[44] he felt that his future was in science fiction and fantasy, a rich genre that was barely being mined by the very medium, motion pictures, that could best present it. For the next ten years he would dwell in this imaginative realm with two feature films and 275 episodes of four hit TV series, at the end of which disaster would strike—in the very best meaning of the word.

---

40   *The Fantasy Worlds of Irwin Allen* is the title of both the book by Jeff Bond and the TV documentary it inspired.

41   TV producer Kevin Burns inherited Allen's paperwork from Allen's widow, Sheila.

42   Author interview July 15, 2022. (see also Richard Chamberlain comments.)

43   AFI catalogue

44   Aubrey Solomon, *Twentieth Century Fox: A Corporate and Financial History,* Lanham, Maryland: Scarecrow Press, 1989.

Chapter 3: Fox and Friend

The Twentieth Century-Fox lot was as famous for its landscaping as for its pictures. A sprawling office and production facility extending from Pico Boulevard in Beverly Hills into adjacent West Los Angeles, the studio was formed in 1935 by Darryl F. Zanuck, who had previously been production VP of Warner Bros., and Joseph Schenck, the producer-brother of Nicholas Schenck, who ran Loew's, Incorporated, which owned MGM. The Zanuck-Schenck company, Twentieth Century Film Corporation, quickly partnered with financier Sidney Kent who had acquired William Fox's floundering Fox Film Corporation in 1930. Zanuck, Schenck, and Kent then invited producer William Goetz to join them. Goetz was more widely known for having married Edith Mayer, the elder daughter of MGM chief Louis B. Mayer. In fact, Mayer became a silent investor in the new studio as much to assure his daughter and son-in-law an income as to cover himself financially in case he was ever fired by Nicholas Schenck, with whom he had a fractious relationship. (This explains why MGM contract stars show up in many Twentieth Century-Fox and even previous Fox films: Mayer was knitting a safety net for himself even at the expense of his own company).

Much emulsion had passed through the gate by the time Irwin Allen arrived at the studio in 1959 to start *The Lost World*. He ate lunch at the Gold Room in the Fox commissary, enjoyed companionship at nearby Hillcrest Country Club, and found a home at the studio's well-appointed production facility.

He immediately set out to construct *Voyage to the Bottom of the Sea* with writing partner Charles Bennett. Their timing couldn't have been better. Although science fiction was (and still is by some) considered a lesser genre, an encouraging succession of box office hits such as *Destination Moon* (1950), *When*

Worlds Collide (1951), *The War of the Worlds* (1953) *Forbidden Planet* (1956), *Journey to the Center of the Earth* (1959), *The Time Machine* (1960), and Allen's own *The Lost World* had accorded sf a veneer of distinction that the studio was willing to finance. But not *that* willing; the average studio budget at the time was $2 million[45] and they gave Irwin only $1.58 million.[46]

Just as *The Animal World* was the film that taught a generation of young movie-goers all about dinosaurs, *Voyage to the Bottom of the Sea* was the film that taught them about the Van Allen radiation belts that embrace the earth. In the Allen-Bennett story the belts have caught on fire for some unknown reason and it becomes the mission of the Seaview nuclear powered submarine, captained by Walter Pidgeon, to explode an atomic bomb at just the right moment in just the right spot to extinguish the belts and, of course, save the earth from being burned to cinders. Shipboard intrigues along the way jeopardize the undertaking which is ultimately a spectacular (for 1961) light show success.

Voyage is a romantic remnant of 1950s attitudes in which the same A-bombs that the Russians were aiming at the United States from around the world could also be used for peace—unless, of course, they were misused by mad scientists to turn small forest creatures into predatory monsters. Directing it himself, Allen makes elegant use Winton C. Hoch's CinemaScope camera that renders the cramped quarters of a submarine as spacious as an ocean liner while still giving a sense of confinement. Having such polished performers as Pidgeon, Joan Fontaine, Robert Sterling, Barbara Eden, Michael Ansara (Eden and Ansara were married in real life), and scene-stealers like Peter Lorre and Henry Daniell, was a bonus. Even if the film's youthful audiences may not have realized the royalty they were watching, Irwin Allen did. He interviewed a thousand stars on his radio show and never tired of their company. Years later he would be able to hire them to

---

45 Joel W. Finler, *The Hollywood Story*, 3d ed. London and New York: Wallflower, 2003.

46 *Aubrey Solomon Twentieth Century Fox: A Corporate and Financial History*, Lanham, Maryland: Scarecrow Press, 1989.

appear in his films instead of having to ask them questions about somebody else's movies.

Voyage is not without its compromises, but who cares? When the Navy declined to cooperate because Allen wouldn't show them the script, Art Director Herman A. Blumenthal used published photographs as well as input from Technical Advisor Fred Zendar to build sets and design the Seaview models.[47] When the results didn't appear flamboyant enough, Allen added Cadillac fins to give the sub a "more rakish appearance and more showmanship."[48] According to the trivia section of the film's Internet Movie database,[49] Fox borrowed elements from other films: the Seaview's first dive is accompanied by the noise of the Martian death ray from Paramount's *War of the Worlds*; props and noises were among those used in *The Fly* (1958); and the whine when the climactic bomb is released is the Batmobile powering up from Fox's TV series (1966). The only thing missing is the Wilhelm scream.[50]

An unusually large release of six hundred prints opened on July 12, 1961 backed by local advertising. A paperback tie-in with Pyramid books was novelized by highly regarded sf writer Theodore Sturgeon and illustrated by Jim Mitchell. For this film, Allen introduced the practice of holding merchandising forums for which he visited eleven key cities, not press conferences but meetings with exhibitors to encourage them to get behind his film. In the years before vast theatre chains such as AMC, Regal, and Cinemark (and, before them, General Cinema, Cineplex-Odeon, Loew's, and National Amusements/Showcase) opened pictures as impersonally as hamburgers at fast-foot outlets, local theatre managers called the shots. Even in the pre-Consent Decree days when studios still owned theatres, it was their local reps who knew their audience habits and were adapt at promoting their attractions. Over two thousand individual managers, bookers,

---

47 *Daily Variety*, December 20, 1960

48 *New York Times*, December 24, 1961

49 https://www.imdb.com/title/tt0055608/trivia/?ref_=tt_ql_trv

50 A stock human injury scream, possibly voiced by actor Sheb Wooley, first used in 1951's *Distant Drums*. You'd know it if you heard it.

and executives heard Allen's pep talk and shook his hand (q.v.), thankful that a producer was getting behind them.[51] The resultant grosses proved the success of his program; the bookings yielded rentals of $7 million, nearly four times the studio's initial investment.[52] It would ultimately lead to the creation of the most successful TV series spin-off of Allen's career.

Allen's 1962 production *Five Weeks in a Balloon*, written by himself and Charles Bennett with a polish by his cousin and longtime associate Al Gail, would be his last theatrical feature for a decade. Developed from one of Jules Verne's earliest (1883) works, it's an odyssey involving a group of travelers floating over Africa. Its episodic structure reflects its origins as a serialized story in Pierre-Jules Hetzel's *Le Magasin d'éducation et de récréation, (the Magazine of Education and Recreation)* and its literary success as the first of Verne's *Extraordinary Voyages* helped establish him as a fantasy novelist.

Five Weeks in a Balloon was not an easy birth. Seven years before Allen decided to produce it, so did actor Tony Curtis. The star and his then-wife Janet Leigh wanted it for their Curtleigh Productions and hired Kathleen Dormer to write the script for himself and Alec Guinness.[53] Others reportedly tried to get a film going until 1961 when Allen announced that he had acquired the rights to the novel.[54] Knowing that there were no rights to secure, producer Bernard Woolner, writer-director Nathan Juran, and Jacques R. Marquette, who also photographed it, made their own version of *Five Weeks* which American International Pictures distributed in December 1961. While the AIP knock-off was still in production, Fox and Allen threatened a lawsuit and, while this didn't stop the competing film, it got the producers to use a different title and to not refer to Jules Verne

---

51   *Boxoffice* magazine, June 26,1961.

52   Solomon, op cit.

53   Philip K. Scheuer, *Los Angeles Times*, November 28, 1955.

54   Howard Thompson, *New York Times*, June 7, 1961. This claim is odd in that the novel had long entered the public domain even though various translations might still have been protected by copyright. In other words, there were no rights to claim.

in connection with it. It was a bluff, but it worked[55] and became part of a two-picture deal. Fox was so hot on the project that the studio's bombastic president Spyros Skouras summoned Allen home from vacation to get right to work. Then, having thus inconvenienced Allen, Skouras postponed the start of production for unspecified reasons.[56]

Among Allen's first casting announcements were Sir Cedric Hardwicke, Red Buttons, and pop singing star Fabian. Barbara Eden, Peter Lorre, Richard Haydn, Henry Danielle, and other Allen regulars would soon join them. Given a generous budget of $2.4 million, Allen at first planned on location filming in Hawaii to substitute for Verne's Africa, then actually went to Kenya to make use of sets still standing from Fox's *The Lion* (Jack Cardiff, 1962) that had just wrapped there.[57] Principal photography was scheduled to begin February 26, 1962 for a very close August 10, 1962 release. Filming wrapped on April 18.[58]

As he had done with the release of *Voyage to the Bottom of the Sea*, Allen again scheduled forums with exhibitors in ten key American cities, seeking to bring them into his fold and get them behind the picture. Allen insisted on including these "grass roots" people on his team, a strategy both he and they never forgot.[59] He even brought along Chester the Chimp (who played "the Duchess" in the picture) to selected cities.[60]

Alas, it was all for naught. *Five Weeks in a Balloon* deflated at the box office, returning only half its budget—$1.2 million—

---

55   Film companies routinely send *pro-forma* cease-and-desist letters to anyone who announces a title similar to one already in their library, not so much to prevent competition as to reinforce their own trademarks. The author has experience with Fox on both sides of this issue. The MPAA (formerly the MPPDA, the Motion Picture Producers and Distributors of America) maintains a Title Registration Bureau where producers can register titles so no one else can use them. It's entirely extralegal (as titles cannot be copyrighted) but survives by mutual consent of its members.

56   *Daily Variety*, August 21, 1961. It's also unusual to hear of Irwin Allen ever taking a vacation.

57   *Daily Variety*, February 23 and 26, 1962.

58   *Daily Variety*, April 19, 1962

59   *Daily Variety*, July 16. 1962.

60   *Daily Variety*, August 3, 1962.

in rentals.[61] Under such circumstances, the second picture in Allen's two-picture deal, *Passage to the End of Space*, died on the launching pad.[62]

Not one to dwell on failure, Allen looked to the future, and the future was television. Little did he know that he would be churning out episodes for the ravenous electronic cyclops for the next ten years.

---

61 Aubrey Solomon, *Twentieth Century Fox: A Corporate and Financial History*, Scarecrow Press, 1989.

62 "Irwin Allen Signs Multiple film Deal," *Los Angeles Times*, June 28, 1961.

Chapter 4: The Earning Channel

Irwin Allen's foray into television was nothing less than a triumph. It also spread science fiction, albeit watered-down science fiction, to a wider audience that, even today, treasures the memories he gave them. At the same time, his TV success fed his desire to return to producing for the big screen. The thirty episodes he produced for *The Time Tunnel*, the eighty-four for *Lost In Space*, the hundred and ten for *Voyage to the Bottom of the Sea*, and the fifty-one for *Land of the Giants*—two hundred and seventy-five in all—form a comforting fabric of memory for an entire generation. They also became a constant reminder to their producer that his talents were too big for the home screen.

Much has been written about each of these series in making-of books, viewing companions, fan celebrations, and episode guides (most notably the exhaustively researched volumes by Marc Cushman and Mark Alfred; see bibliography). The best of them are meticulous and passionate, and this chapter will not attempt to compete. Instead, it will view Allen's foursome in terms of how they led to *The Poseidon Adventure* and *The Towering Inferno*.

For starters, it seemed natural for *Voyage to the Bottom of the Sea* to become a weekly TV series. After all, the Seaview, having saved the world in 1961, could easily turn its missiles toward more mundane earthly crises each week starting in 1964. Seasoned actor Richard Basehart replaced Walter Pidgeon as Admiral Harriman Nelson and David Hedison slipped into the role of Captain Lee Crane that was vacated by Robert Sterling. Others in the cast (replacing Joan Fontaine, Barbara Eden, Peter Lorre, and Michael Ansara) included Robert Dowdell, Del Monroe, Richard Bull, and Paul Carr. Operating from stories and teleplays by Allen and thirty-eight other writers, including buddy Charles Bennett and cousin Al Gail, *Voyage* lasted four seasons.

"I liked him, but we were always arguing," said David Hedison, who had turned down *The Lost World* and reluctantly agreed to co-star in *Voyage* on advice of his agent and the chance to work with Richard Basehart. But he remained concerned that the show was relentlessly foreboding. "I wanted humor in the scenes between the admiral and the captain," he said, "but Irwin would have none of it. He just knew that he always wanted the action to be very grim and very solid and very tense, and that's what he got."[63]

Always conscious of costs, for the TV series Allen repurposed some of the footage he had originally shot for the feature, scanning-and-panning its wide CinemaScope frame to fit on the nearly square television tube. For scenes where the Seaview was buffeted by depth charges, giant sea creatures, and other menaces and the crew was tossed back and forth, Allen had everyone simply throw themselves to one side of the set while the camera tilted in the other direction. To make sure everyone moved and tilted at the same time, he would take a stick and bang on a bucket. (By the time he made *The Towering Inferno*, he'd switched from hitting a bucket with a stick to firing a pistol.) He was still vexed, however, by water shots that looked, at times, like they were shot in a bath tub no matter how much water Fox's backlot tank held or how big the submarine model was. *Voyage* lasted an impressive hundred and ten episodes from September 14, 1964 to March 31, 1968.

If Allen is loved and remembered for any single television achievement, however, it is *Lost In Space*. The continuing storyline, which would go on for eighty-four episodes over three years, debuted on September 8, 1965. By this time, Allen had 225 people on his payroll and was occupying two of Fox's soundstages, not to mention his own large, well-appointed offices on the Pico Boulevard studio lot. Promoting the show in advance

---

63   Interviewed in *The Fantasy Worlds of Irwin Allen*, Van Ness Films/SciFi Channel, 1995.

of its debut, Allen called it "science fact" instead of "science fiction" (because "science fact" could actually happen today) and boasted that "*Space* will be the first primetime cliffhanger in the history of TV. The whole series is a cliffhanger. We will leave them (our series family) hanging in space and resolve it the next week, then get them in worse difficulties that week."[64]

Lost n Space is unashamedly inspired by Johann David Wyss's 1812 novel, *The Swiss Family Robinson.* Its premise is that, by 1997, the Bomb is no longer Mankind's prime threat to survival but has been outdistanced by another kind of explosion, population. The Robinson family is chosen by a worldwide computer system to venture forth and seek other worlds, with the rest of humanity presumably to follow. It's a little like *When Worlds Collide* without the colliding. The core explorer group was Dr. John Robinson (Guy Williams), his wife Maureen (June Lockhart), their daughters Judy and Penny (Marta Kristen and Angela Cartwright, respectively), their young son Will (Bill Mumy), and an unrelated member, pilot Major Don West (Mark Goddard). Launched in suspended animation, they head for the planet (sic) Alpha Centauri but are deflected by a meteor encounter to an unknown planet where they are awakened and must survive.

Not everybody was on board at the start. Said Mark Goddard, "I just thought it was going to be like a kid's cartoon show" but then changed his mind after a few episodes when he realized, "This was a science fiction adventure that was exciting. It wasn't the cartoon that I thought it would be."[65]

At first, yes. Originally designed as a serious story of survival on a hostile world, it was changed at network request to be more in keeping with CBS's family hour obligations. Responding to network demands, Allen added two characters: Robot Model B-9 and a creepy, meddlesome stowaway named Dr. Zachary Smith who seemed to spend an unhealthy amount of time hanging around young Will.

---

64 Dave Kaufman, *Variety*, June 1, 1965
65 Interviewed in *The Fantasy Worlds of Irwin Allen*, Van Ness Films/SciFi Channel, 1995.

"He was more of a father figure to the boy than the father was," said co-writer Shimon Wincelberg."[66] Added Jonathan Harris, who played the flamboyant Smith, he decided to add humor to his interpretation because he knew that, otherwise, his character would be eliminated after five or six episodes. "And unemployment is so boring." When Allen caught on to what he was doing, rather than become upset, he told the actor, "Do more."[67]

It was a wise decision ratings-wise but it dented, if not broke, Allen's heart. He had wanted to make a serious study of a marooned family more in keeping with his love of adventure; the network wanted something with monsters and interpersonal conflict, and how much conflict can there be within a family that was chosen by computer because they get along so well with each other?

Produced on a lavish $700,000 budget—supposedly the largest ever spent at the time for a TV pilot—*Lost in Space's* first episode, "No Place to Hide," was shot in black-and-white except for the effects scenes which Allen went to the expense of filming in color in case he ever wanted to use them elsewhere or if the show changed to color. Allen directed the pilot himself, and that version was never aired—only the recut with Robot and Smith added went out—and it was considered lost until 1990.

Allen described *Lost in Space* as being for families, "because you couldn't keep the kids away with a baseball bat, so we had damned well better write adult stories to get maximum appeal." When queried how he could fulfill his promise of adding guest stars to a show set on an isolated world with no outsiders beyond the main cast, Allen playfully deflected the question by saying, "Don't ask me."[68]

The year after *Lost in Space* launched on September 8, 1965, Allen debuted his third series, *The Time Tunnel*. It was announced with a January 3, 1966 squib in *Variety* under the unfortunate (or,

---

66 Interviewed in *The Fantasy Worlds of Irwin Allen*, Van Ness Films/SciFi Channel, 1995.

67 Interviewed in *The Fantasy Worlds of Irwin Allen*, Van Ness Films/SciFi Channel, 1995.

68 Dave Kaufman, *Variety*, June 1, 1965

knowing *Variety*, probably not) headline, "Irwin Allen Starts Boring TV 'Tunnel.'" The pilot would shoot for twenty days at Westwood Studios with location work in Arizona.

Time Tunnel was more in line with true science fiction and dared to challenge what's known as the "grandfather paradox,"[69] namely that going back in time can have cumulative effects as the years pass. But why let the prime directive get in the way of a good story? Doctors Tony Newman (James Darren) and Doug Phillips (Robert Colbert) are two scientists whose experiments with time travel go awry and send them to various moments in history where they interact with people and try to return home, with Whit Bissell as Lt. General Heywood Kirk, their crusty supervisor, waiting for them. The cliffhanger device, which Allen had come to use as a viewer magnet, was from a story he conceived with Harold Jack Bloom and Shimon Wincelberg and a teleplay by Bloom and Wincelberg. Bloom never wrote for the series again; Wincelberg wrote seven episodes.[70] Adding to the scientific verisimilitude was an actual Burroughs B205 computer purchased used from the United States Air Force.

The advantages of working at a major studio showed up on the screen every week. Whenever it was necessary to go into the past, there was always something lying around the scene dock. Producer Allen saved a fortune by reusing old props and pieces of sets that were in storage from past Fox pictures. He even found a way to use clips from the studio's bygone black-and-white movies by tinting it to conjure the past. Such cost-cutting skills held down the budget, but to little avail; *The Time*

69　More specifically, if you go back in time and kill your grandfather, it means you never would have been born, and thus could not go back in time to kill your grandfather. *Star Trek* creator Gene Roddenberry acknowledged this by establishing the Prime Directive forbidding any Star Fleet ship that happened to go back in time from affecting any event or person while they were there, even though they knew its historical effect, good or bad (viz Harlan Ellison's script, "City on the Edge of Forever"). A corollary is the "Butterfly Effect" in which even the smallest event – say, removing a grain of sand or stepping off a wooded path in the past – can compound into huge consequences in the future, given the myriad variables in the flow of life. And now back to our book.

70　*Variety*, January 3, 1966.

Tunnel debuted September 13, 1966 on ABC-TV but its clock ran out on April 7, 1967 after thirty episodes. The cancellation stung; despite good reviews, the show had received only mild ratings. Even though everybody wanted it to be continued, the Fox bean counters would only allow it to do so if Allen could trim its budget by one-third on top of his already astute parsimony. Allen refused to accede, so Tony and Doug became forever stuck in time.

By March 1966 Allen had three shows on network and was spending $12 million of Fox's money every year to make them. Despite the failure of *The Time Tunnel,* the studio was ecstatic and so were the teams of writers and crew members churning them out, not to mention the casts. Allen boasted of this to *Variety* and tipped that he had a project lined up with *Voyage* actor Alfred Ryder (Dr. Krueger and Dr. Bergstrom) who, he said—in a rather confusing quote—he had cast in a theatrical project "for release by Fox abroad on *Voyage*" without him offering further details.[71]

In 1968 he embarked on *Land of the Giants*. The concept was simple, if devoid of scientific accuracy: the Spindrift, a transport ship in earth orbit, is sucked into a magnetic field that sends it to another world where everything is twelve times the size of anything on earth. The crew must keep from being squished by the "giants" who inhabit this unnamed planet until they can build a radio to signal home for help. Many of the oversized props were rented from Universal Pictures who had kept them in storage after they filmed *The Incredible Shrinking Man* in 1957. Shot in color, which increased the cost and immensely complicated the optical effects, *Giants* lasted two seasons and fifty-one episodes from September 22, 1968 to March 22, 1970.

At his busiest time during this period, Allen had four shows going—five, counting Irwin Allen. As a cynical Morton Moss wrote in the *Los Angeles Herald-Examiner*, "Allen is a showman who

---

71 *Variety,* March 30, 1966. Unless this refers to the theatrical release of two or more edited *Voyage* episodes (a common practice), there is no indication whether it came about.

likes to showcase his series of TV series and movies. He also likes to showcase himself." Likening him to P. T. Barnum, Moss quoted Allen, "I do these shows for money but every show originated from a personal dream. My dreams are wild and wooly. My subconscious forces these dreams on me, and I have the most commercial subconscious in town. Even my dreams have commercials." Zinged a skeptical Moss, "Not being Allen's psychiatrist, we can't vouch for the authenticity of the dream material. But, even an amateur in mental therapy could guess that Allen is less prone to suffer from an Oedipus complex than to turn a profit on it." Repeating Allen's report that he had just closed a three-picture deal with Joseph E. Levine's Embassy Pictures, only one of which was for science fiction, and Allen's remark that "reality is stranger than fiction," Moss concludes, "Allen may have dreamed of being Lost in Space but he's never at a loss for a word, even if it is partly borrowed."[72]

What Allen thought of the article is not recorded—certainly his clipping service sent it to him—but one doesn't have to read between Moss's snarky lines to see that Allen's tireless self-promoting could rub people the wrong way. Very likely he followed the maxim, "never mind what they write as long as they spell your name right" in that any coverage outside of an obituary is publicity gold.

Forget the pundits; Allen was having a ball. Single and happily consumed by a career that actually paid off, he worked in a brightly colored office surrounded by an entourage. He tooled around town in a two-toned light and dark chocolate Rolls-Royce, got to wear comfortable clothing (to hide his bulk) in an age when producers still wore suits, and was, in the words of columnist Jack Hellman, "a one-man conglomerate."[73]

There was only one thing he wanted that he didn't already have.

Movies.

---

72 Morton Moss, *Los Angeles Herald-Examiner*, July 3, 1969.
73 Jack Hellman, "Light and Airy," *Variety*, July 15, 1968.

Chapter 4 Sidebar: But Is It Science Fiction?

Strictly speaking, Irwin Allen didn't make science fiction. He made science fantasy. It's a stuffy distinction, but even he would admit that his tastes ran more to action adventure than consciousness-expanding metaphysics. Science fiction involves speculation based on current or future science or technology. In sf (the preferred abbreviation; never "sci-fi") story and science are wedded; if you take out the science, the story falls apart.

"Science fiction is the art of the possible," said Ray Bradbury, one of its most-honored icons. "Fantasy is the art of the impossible. Science fiction, again, is the history of ideas, and they're always ideas that work themselves out and become real and happen in the world."[74]

"I have a specific definition of science fiction," adds David Gerrold (*Star Trek*: "The Trouble with Tribbles"). "The story is rooted in a scientific possibility or extrapolation. [Isaac] Asimov's robots are science fiction. Hal Clement wrote science fiction. Robert L. Forward wrote science fiction. Arthur C. Clarke wrote science fiction. There's real science in science fiction."[75]

Perhaps this is why Harlan Ellison (*A Boy and His Dog*, "I Have No Mouth, And I Must Scream") bristled when people said he wrote science fiction. "I've always hated the phrase *science fiction* 'cuz I don't write science fiction," he said, "It's a misnomer. Robert Heinlein created the term *speculative fiction*, which I always thought was closer to it." In a phrase, Ellison regarded the few sf stories he wrote as "what if?" stories.[76] Nevertheless, Ellison wrote a script for *Voyage to the Bottom of the Sea* (about which more later).

---

74 *Christian Science Monitor*, November 13, 1980.

75 "Thinking About Science Fiction," April 25, 2019. https://medium.com/@davidgerrold/thinking-about-science-fiction-dd48e8473532

76 Interview with the author for *A Lit Fuse*, Massachusetts: NESFA Press, 2017.

Although there are clearly amounts of science in the work that Allen produced for both small and large screen, one has to admit that they are more in the line of action-adventure with scientific overlays. The Seaview of *Voyage to the Bottom of the Sea* is a nuclear submarine just like the real ones that the U.S. Navy already had patrolling the seas. *Lost in Space* is a domestic comedy-drama set on a world that most of the time could just as well be an isolated earth community. *Land of the Giants* involves issues of mass and gravity that defy physics, but so what? Only *The Time Tunnel*, impossible as time travel is, depends on science to trigger its stories.

It's best to regard Allen as a storyteller, not a scientist, and his shows and films as entertainment, not a physics exam.

Chapter 4 Sidebar: Flight of the Seaview

No story of the *Voyage to the Bottom of the Sea* television series would be complete without mention of Harlan Ellison. Ellison, the multi-award-winning speculative fiction (sic) writer, was a hot TV property in the 1960s, penning episodes for such top shows as *Burke's Law, The Outer Limits, The Alfred Hitchcock Hour, Star Trek*, and *The Man From U.N.C.L.E.* In 1964 he was hired to write an episode for *Voyage* titled called "The Price of Doom." The plot is nominally about an aggressive form of Antarctic sea plankton that eats people, but it's the story behind the episode that has become the stuff of legend. It has to do with the heavy hand of ABC network censorship in the form of one Adrian Samish (now deceased).

Ellison turned in his treatment—a prose precursor to writing the script—on April 20, 1964 while the episode bore the ironic but apt title "Mealtime." He followed it with his first draft script at the beginning of May. By the time he submitted his "final draft" on May 21, it was being called "The Price of Doom." The title was prescient.

Enter Adrian Samish, the universally despised ABC censor. On network TV it was the job of the censor—euphemistically called "continuity acceptance"—to weed out and correct anything that might run afoul of "standards and practices" that were monitored by the FCC that might offend viewers. Among Samish's notes, which Ellison considered capricious, were instructions to change a character's name to sound less British, alter a female character's hair color, and say that the villain, who had been on the Seaview for months, should suddenly be revealed to have been wearing a face mask. Ellison countered every one of Samish's notes by explaining how they wouldn't work. But it was when Samish ordered, "You'll do it! Writers are toadies" that Ellison—sitting at one end of a long table flanked by Allen and the show's staff and seething at every condescending comment—lost his famously fragile temper. He leapt onto the table, ran toward Samish full-bore with his fist extended and ready to slug him. En route, however, he slipped on some papers, fell to his stomach, and skidded right into Samish's throat. Samish tumbled backward in his chair, dislodging a heavy model of the Seaview from its mooring on the wall. The Seaview dropped straight onto the censor, breaking his pelvis. In the melee, Ellison was escorted, still fuming, to a side office and held there until studio medics carted Samish away.

"Irwin Allen's head exploded," Ellison recalled for his 2017 biography *A Lit Fuse.* "He didn't know whether to shit or wind his watch." For this and other reasons, little of what Ellison wrote wound up in the finished episode, which story editor William Welch and associate story editor (and Allen crony) Al Gail probably had a hand in rewriting. The episode is the first time that Ellison applied what would become his well-known pseudonym, "Cordwainer Bird" (that appeared in the credits as Cord Wainer Bird).

For years the story has been disputed as Ellison's fantasy and has even veered into conjecture that the argumentative writer attacked Irwin Allen himself. The latter is not true, but the former begs examination.

Ellison was asked about the incident by Elliot Brown in *The Comics Journal* (#53, Winter 1980) and insisted, "No! I never touched Irwin Allen! It was the head of ABC Network Continuity that I punched. Irwin Allen was just sitting to the right. Yeah, well, that's absolutely true. And actually, I would have kicked him in the face. See, I didn't mean to punch him in the face, I meant to kick him in the face, but I ran down this table and it was a 10-foot-long table and it had been highly polished and I slipped and fell and I slid on my stomach and when I came at this guy I hit him and caught him in the mouth and he went over backwards and fell off his chair and this model of the Seaview fell off the wall and broke his pelvis. That's what happened."

But here's something confusing. Writing on *ComicMix* on December 3, 2007 ("Speaking Ill of the Dead"), Mike Gold says, "The subsequent lawsuit was settled out of court." Yet no evidence of a lawsuit could be located when *A Lit Fuse* was being researched, nor was any report of a civil suit for assault and battery.

As for Samish's reputation, Ellison wasn't alone in his enmity. An unidentified contributor on the Irwin Allen Wiki[77] wrote, "Harlan had a right to be angry. Adrian Samish has been called a total terror by *Outer Limits* director Gerd Oswald [and] was thrown out of Joseph Stefano's office." The blogger then quotes Robert Payne, an assistant to Ben Brady, who took over [producing] *The Outer Limits*, as saying, "Samish was a fellow who could, quote, command. He was one of those schizophrenic network personalities who could be charming, generous, and wonderful one moment, and the next, be willing to conduct a personality castration of you right in front of God and everybody. He produced

---

77 As of this writing: https://irwinallentvseries.fandom.com/wiki/VOYAGE_
TO_THE_BOTTOM_OF_THE_SEA-THE_PRICE_OF_DOOM

half the shows at ABC [most of them 1974-5] but never wrote or directed one damned teleplay."[78]

So, then, did Harlan Ellison actually attack Adrian Samish? In all probability, yes. Did he go after him verbally? No question; Ellison's wrath was not only toxic, it was breathtakingly articulate. Did he skid down a table, send the Seaview flying, and break the man's pelvis? Possible but not causal. Ellison was short (5'5") and often took to standing on platforms. But did he connect physically with Samish? It has been suggested that Samish pushed his chair back to avoid Ellison and brought the Seaview down upon himself, which has a delicious symbolism. Besides, after seeing "The Price of Doom," he deserved it. Whatever the scenario, Ellison was quickly banished from both Fox and ABC.[79] Samish ultimately quit the network and went to work for Quinn Martin at Warner Bros., allegedly as a favor between Martin and Allen.

At QM he made people equally miserable. *Sic semper ad censores.*

---

78 To be fair, IMDb credits him with creating the 1954 soap operas *First Love* and *A Time to Live*, a rewrite on the 1971 TV movie *Travis Logan D.A.*, and a story on a 1973 *Barnaby Jones* episode.

79 Ellison had submitted a pitch for ABC's *Batman* series and was in producer William Dozier's office when Samish phoned to report that he had approved all of the next season's episodes except Ellison's.

Chapter 5: *Poseidon* Sets the Template

The film that started it all almost didn't get made.[80] Published January 1, 1969 by Coward-McCann Books, *The Poseidon Adventure*, by the prolific former sports writer-turned-novelist Paul Gallico, attracted little attention. Dismissed by the *New York Times* as "a *Grand Hotel* full of shipboard dossiers," it came to the attention of Avco-Embassy Pictures as a routine submission for a movie sale. At the time, Avco-Embassy was flush with income from *The Graduate*, the 1967 Mike Nichols hit that Joseph E. Levine had produced for his own company, Embassy Pictures, which he then sold to the Avco Corporation. Believing that every year would be like 1967, Avco paid Levine $40 million for Embassy, attached their name, and started making plans.[81]

Irwin Allen, whose career had been primarily at Twentieth Century-Fox Television, took his Kent Productions to Avco-Embassy and signed a three-picture deal, the first result of which was to be *The Poseidon Adventure*, which Allen himself had optioned. The first writer he hired to adapt Gallico's novel was Wendell Mayes, a former TV writer whose first feature credit was with Billy Wilder on *The Spirit of St. Louis* but who subsequently languished in potboilers until Otto Preminger gave him *Anatomy of a Murder*. There followed *In Harm's Way*, *Advise and Consent*, and *Von Ryan's Express* (shared with Joseph Landon, Joseph Westheimer, and Saul David, the latter two uncredited). Mayes was an expert at "breaking the spine" of a novel, in other words,

---

80   Some pin the start of disaster film cycle to 1970's *Airport*, but that was arguably a danger drama in the mold of *The High and the Mighty* (1954); granted, it's a judgment call.

81   Stanley Penn, "Avco to Buy Embassy Pictures from Levine for $40 Million of Common, Preferred Stock," *Wall Street Journal*, May 6, 1968. The headstrong Levine lasted four years, then departed to form his own company, Joseph E. Levine Presents.

finding a through-line to the story that would play on the screen. Unfortunately for *Poseidon*, it was the wrong through-line.

"I'll tell you what was attractive about *The Poseidon Adventure*," Mayes told interviewer Rul Nogueira, "the money I was offered. I knew that it was going to be a big, bad, popular motion picture. I was the first writer on it. After I did a couple of rewrites, I asked the producer, Irwin Allen, to please relieve me of the job. I had done all I could. Then he brought in Stirling Silliphant. Stirling worked on it and changed it quite a bit, enough so that I think he got first credit."[82]

Silliphant had a field day. "This one was far easier [than *The Towering Inferno*]," he said, "all due to Paul Gallico. *Poseidon* was a straight-out story with some (because of Paul) well-written, flesh-and-blood characters. The narrative line is simple: a passenger liner turns hull up and is sinking by the bow, its time afloat unknown, but hardly more than a matter of hours. A group of survivors has to work its way UP toward what had previously been the bottom and, if they can achieve that level, attempt to break through the hull before the liner sinks. The group more or less remained intact, despite arguments among them, chiefly a difference of opinion between the Ernie Borgnine character and the Gene Hackman character as to which way is the only way to survival. So, no, it was far less *Grand Hotel* underwater than *Towering Inferno* was *Grand Hotel* in a burning high-rise.

"The matter of making the characters empathetic was not a problem because I had a simple and central conflict going between Borgnine and Hackman. In their conflict they exposed their own fears—and therefore their humanity. And as this impacted on the several other characters we inevitably had to see them as facets of ourselves. And how can you go wrong with an actress of the brilliance of Shelley Winters whose chubby rump has to be pushed upward—and her face of complaint at such a rude contact—and

---

82 "Wendell Mayes: The Jobs Poured Over Me," *Backstory 3*, Patrick McGilligan, editor, California: University of California Press, 1997. Writers Guild rules normally accord screen credit in the order in which successive writers work on a script. *Poseidon* was an anomaly. It reads "Screenplay by Stirling Silliphant and Wendell Mayes," the word *and* indicating that they did not work as a team.

then when she has to dive and swim a hazardous course underwater in her bloomers—and dies in the arms of her husband before they can get to Israel—come on, that's really snatching candy from a baby."[83]

It was Silliphant's rewrite that got the green light for the film, which carried a $4.7 million dollar budget. Unable to swing that amount, Avco-Embassy allowed Allen to take the project to his old home studio, Twentieth Century-Fox, to set it up there.

At the time, Fox was still reeling from the costly disaster of 1963's *Cleopatra* (which had forced them to sell off their backlot to developers who turned it into what is now Century City). Although such hits as *Planet of the Apes, Valley of the Dolls*, and *Butch Cassidy and the Sundance Kid* had brought in big money, a succession of expensive flops like *Tora, Tora, Tora, Doctor Doolittle, Star!*, and *Hello Dolly* pulled them back toward the financial abyss. The only way to prevent tumbling in was to cancel their biggest-budget film, and this was *Poseidon*.

There was some risk in doing so. Allen, director Ronald Neame, Production Designer William Creber, and Fox's immense construction crew had been hard at work for months preparing for the shoot, which was scheduled to start in two weeks. In addition, many of the actors were pay-or-play, meaning that they had to be paid regardless of whether they were used or the picture was made. All told, if the studio canceled the picture, they would have to absorb all the costs to date. But that's just what they decided to do in a hastily arranged meeting at which they gave Allen the courtesy of telling him to his face.

Why Fox made this decision is baffling. Allen was their golden ticket. His four TV series were a Fort Knox that would, even

---

83 Nat Segaloff, *Stirling Silliphant: The Fingers of God*, Albany, Georgia: BearManor Media, 2013. Notably, in Paul Gallico's novel, Winters' character (Belle Rosen) dies long after her swim yet only moments before the group's rescue. Moreover, Gene Hackman's character (Rev. Scott) gratuitously leaps to death after blasphemously daring God to swap his life for the others—not, as in the film, after heroically shutting a steam value that blocks their escape. These changes, which tighten both drama and character, typify Silliphant's skills.

though deficit-financed, generate years of continuing income through worldwide reruns and syndication.

In some tellings of the *Poseidon* story (there are several versions, all of them sympathetic to Allen), he was on the verge of tears. Not only was his picture killed, so were his feature film ambitions. Not giving up, he got the executives to admit that his film had commercial potential, just that they couldn't afford it. This was hope enough to send him into salesman mode. The next day, his tears replaced by resolve, he returned to Fox and got management to commit two million dollars by promising them that he would contribute the rest of the money. What Fox did not know (or perhaps it was a double bluff) was that he didn't have it.

The Hillcrest Country Club at 10000 West Pico Boulevard is less than a mile from Fox's studios at 10201 West Pico in Beverly Hills. Built in 1920 by LA's Jewish community when anti-Semitism barred them from joining the city's existing Protestant country clubs, it is a haven for show business movers and shakers. Emboldened with Fox's promise of partial financing, Allen raced to Hillcrest and immediately found several of his colleagues, including producer/exhibitor Sherrill Corwin (whom he knew from RKO) and independent producer Steve Broidy, playing gin rummy. Allen asked if any of them happened to have $2.7 million to invest, and pitched them *Poseidon*. Corwin and Broidy said yes, shook hands with Allen, and told him, "Now get out and let us finish our game!"[84]

Their percentage of the film's eventual worldwide gross of $84,563,118[85] (yielding an estimated $42 million in returns) made them even richer.

But even with a budget, Allen still had to make the movie. His team was in place. His helmer was cinematographer-turned-director Ronald Neame, a Britton known for his taste and composure. He would need both in the course of production. Allen

---

84   This legendary story may well be embroidered as Allen had a morbid fear of handshakes (q.v.)

85   IMDb

was also fortunate in hiring Shelley Winters and Ernest Borgnine, both of whom were Oscar®-winners. Gene Hackman, at the time, was known as a working actor but not a star; he had made a few films, including *Bonnie and Clyde* and *The French Connection*. It was during the water-soaked shoot of *Poseidon* that he won his Oscar® as *The French Connection*'s Popeye Doyle. By the time *Poseidon* was released, he was a star but Allen had had to pay him only an actor's salary.

Shelley Winters was already a star, and an eccentric one. Ronald Neame recalled a brouhaha when they were ready to shoot Belle diving through a submerged compartment to find the engine room. "In the script," he recalled, "she says to Gene Hackman 'Please let me do this one, please let me dive in and go and look for the engine room because I'm a professional swimmer. I'm a life saver. I can do this. Please let me do something.' And she gets stuck, and then he goes in and rescues her. Gene came to me two days before we were going to shoot the scene and said, 'You know, Ronnie, this doesn't work. I wouldn't let that old woman dive in like that. I mean, there's no way I'd let her do that.' And I said, 'Well, what do we do, Gene?' He said, 'It's simple. I won't let her dive in. *I* dive in and *I* get trapped, and she comes in and rescues me.' I thought, 'What a good idea.' So, of course, we presented it to Shelley. She said, 'I only decided to do this film because of this scene. You are destroying the scene, you are destroying my part, and I will not have it,' and she walked off the set. You can imagine that was a bit of a problem. But an hour later she came back and said, 'Well, I'm ready. Is everybody else ready?' and it had a happy ending."[86] (It was also noteworthy that Hackman was content to be rescued rather than do the rescuing. This is a level of understanding of a film's bigger picture that separates actors, which he is, from stars, which he became.)

As an old pro, Neame knew how to deal with producers and survived the Irwin Allen experience dispassionately. "Irwin liked

---

86 Interview, *Hell Under Water, Fire in the Sky,* op cit. Both the Gallico book and the third revised shooting final script dated March 24, 1972 have Belle diving first and Scott saving her. The film reverses this.

everybody to think that he ran everything, that he was boss-man in charge of everything," Neame said, smiling. "He was also a frustrated director. He liked every shot on the storyboard and he'd put the drawings all around the wall. When people came to visit him, he'd say, 'You see? We plan everything ahead.' I fought Irwin on that. I dislike storyboards. I won't use them. And I won. But I didn't completely win because, the next day when we had the rushes on the screen, he would send his sketch artists into the theatre and they would draw my shots and put them 'round his wall, because he had such an ego that he couldn't bear the idea that he wasn't in charge of everything." Neame paused. "However, I forgive him. I'm still here and he isn't."[87]

Allen filled *Poseidon* with stunts and hired the industry's best stunt performers to carry them out supervised by Stunt Coordinator Paul Stader (who would work on *The Towering Inferno*). For a stunt in which a man was to fall "up" into a glass skylight, he demanded that it be done in one shot starting with a close-up. Stunt performer Ernie F. Orsatti was hired to perform what has become one of the greatest gags in movie history.

"I was working in a Mobil gas station not too far from Twentieth Century-Fox," Orsatti said. "My mother called Irwin Allen, who was an old family friend, and found out he was doing a movie. Sure enough, they called me for a part, a small part. The part called for that character to fall through the skylight when the ship turned upside-down. He said, 'Could you do it? We'd like everybody to do their own stunts.' The fall was a little weird. To fall straight-away without turning your lead or pointing your head to know when you're going to hit—falling blind. When I got there, I was so green, having never done this, I had never bothered to check what was going to be my catcher, what I was going to hit—and they wanted it to look like the guy hit solid—and it did. Then the surprising part was they'd never done anything like that and the production manager gave me $150. I was expecting something a lot bigger, but it made the Smithsonian Institute,

---

87 Neame died in 2010 at age 99. Interview from *Hell Under Water, Fire in the Sky,* op cit.

and *Maxim Magazine* voted it their favorite number one Hollywood stunt of all time, so. . .but at a hundred and fifty bucks, it was famous."[88]

The Poseidon Adventure was released on December 12, 1972. The film that Fox half-bailed on wound up saving their corporate assets. "When, week after week, in London I would buy *Variety* and there we were at the top, the number one picture," recalled Neame. "Not for weeks but for months. It appeals to the eleven-year-olds up to fifteen-year-olds. They were the letters I would get."[89]

Said Stella Stevens, who starred as Ernest Borgnine's wife, "There's not another movie like it anywhere. It was totally unique."[90]

At last count, the picture is the eighty-ninth top-grossing film of all time and, despite one forgettable sequel (1979) and a half-hearted television remake (2005), it is still remembered as the disaster picture that lit the fuse that would burn all the way to *The Towering Inferno*.

---

88 Interviewed in *Hell Under Water, Fire in the Sky*, op cit. There may be a little embroidery in this recollection. Orsatti (son of St. Louis Cardinals "Gashouse Gang" first baseman and stunt performer, as well as Irwin Allen's former employer, Ernie Orsatti) had already done stunt work in *The Green Berets* (1968) and *The Star-Spangled Girl* (1971). But it's still a great story. Orsatti died in 2020 at age 80 following a stroke.
89 Interviewed in *Hell Under Water, Fire in the Sky*, op cit.
90 ibid

The U.S.S. Poseidon (played by the Queen Mary, which was drydocked in Long Beach, California as a tourist attraction) is about to be retired after she makes one last trip from New York to Athens where its new owner, Linarcos (Fred Sadoff) runs his fleet. Linarcos is in such a rush to get home that he forbids Captain Harrison (Leslie Nielsen) from taking on ballast that would steady the vessel.

In short order most of the main characters are introduced: Reverend Scott (Gene Hackman) has been exiled to Africa by his church for his activist views. Manny Rosen (Jack Albertson) and his wife Belle (Shelley Winters) are heading to Israel to see their grandchildren. Mike and Linda Rogo (Ernest Borgnine and Stella Stevens)—he a police detective and she a former hooker—are out for a vacation cruise. Siblings Susan and Robin Shelby (Pamela Sue Martin and Eric Shea) are joining their parents in Europe. Clothing salesman James Martin (Red Buttons) is trying to rest.

On the stroke of midnight, during a New Year's Eve party, the Poseidon is hit by a tidal wave that flops the huge vessel upside-down, throwing the passengers, who are celebrating in the ballroom, topsy-turvy. Many are crushed or flung to their deaths against the "ceiling," which becomes the floor. When the chaos settles, Reverend Scott realizes that it's only a matter of time before the vessel sinks. He rallies the throngs to follow him "up" to what is now the bottom hull of the ship. It's risky, but it's the only chance for survival. The Rogos, the Rosens, Martin, and the Shelby kids follow him along with Acres, a steward (Roddy McDowall) who knows the ship intimately, and singer Nonnie Parry (Carol Lynley) whose brother has died on the bandstand. In short order, those who decided to wait for rescue in the ballroom die when water floods in, and the Scott party barely manages to escape through a bulkhead door.

The desperate group encounters peril after peril. Acres is thrown to his death when one of the ship's engine explodes and knocks him off a ladder in the ventilation shaft. The party needs to find the engine room, and with it the propeller shaft, but when they encounter the ship's doctor Caravello (Jan Arvan) leading a party in another direction, Rogo demands Scott prove himself. He does, but then the group is separated from the engine room by a flooded compartment. Belle, who says she was a swimming champion years ago, argues to go underwater and string a rope to guide the rest through the murky water. Scott refuses and goes himself but becomes ensnared on the way. Belle dives in and rescues him. Both Scott and Belle make it through. She dies of a heart attack, but not before giving Scott a pendant and asking him to tell her husband to bring it for her to Israel.

The group makes it through oil fires to the thinnest part of the ship's hull, the propeller shaft junction, but another explosion knocks Linda off the path to her death in the fiery waters. Suddenly, a steam pipe bursts, blocking the remaining survivors' escape route. Scott jumps into the breach to shut it and does so, knowing that he will fall to his death. Now there is a tapping on the outside of the hull and soon a torch begins cutting through the metal. A rescue team has arrived to save the six remaining travelers. A helicopter hovers above the stern of the Poseidon, lifting the group to safety as the huge ship slips beneath the surface of the drink.

Main differences between novel and film:
- When the ship's generators blow, the escape party is in darkness and must use flashlights for much of their trek. In the film, the lights stay on.
- The Shelbys travel as a family and the parents' marriage breaks down as they work toward the ship's bottom. Young Robin Shelby goes off to the bathroom, never to be seen again.

- Linda Rogo becomes infatuated with Reverend Frank "Buzz" Scott.
- It is Linda Rogo, not her husband Mike, who rebels at the delay and, in trying to find her own escape route, falls and is impaled on a torn girder.
- Belle Rosen goes first and finds the engine room but dies of a heart attack much later when the oxygen supply in the propeller shaft gets low while they wait for rescue.
- When all looks darkest, Reverend Scott curses God and kills himself, traumatizing Mary Kinsale, a single woman, who claims that the two of them were to be married.
- When the group is rescued by a German tramp steamer they are surprised to see other survivors who have made it, having followed the doctor after all.
- After the Poseidon finally sinks, everyone goes his, her, and their separate ways. The film ends before this happens and the end titles appear.

Chapter 6: Two Books, One Film

Coincidences happen in publishing as in movies but, unlike movies, the critics don't write Sunday pieces pronouncing it a trend. Under copyright law the only way to protect an idea is to set it down in permanent form; the more elaborate its articulation, the more protection in cases of suspected plagiarism. There is no indication that the authors of *The Tower* (Richard Martin Stern) or *The Glass Inferno* (Thomas N. Scortia and Frank M. Robinson) ever met, talked with, or knew each other, at least not while they were writing their separate books. It may simply be that, if one decides to write about a fire in a high rise building, the same plot requirements almost automatically present themselves. Looking at it through a different window, both books follow a well-worn formula—group jeopardy—and it falls to the authors to make the predictable seem spontaneous. Potboiler books and action movies have that much in common: you must know where they're going without seeing how they're getting there.

The Tower changed the direction of Richard Martin Stern's writing career. Starting as a novelist comparatively late at age forty-three with *The Bright Road to Fear* (1958), which won him the 1959 Edgar Allen Poe award from the Mystery Writers of America as best first novel, he followed it the next year with four short novels collected under the title *Suspense*. Stern's output continued with one new title almost every year focusing on private investigators and procedurals. In 1971 he created Johnny Ortiz, a part-Apache police detective with the Santo Cristo, New Mexico force, in the novel *Death in the Snow*, kicking off a six-book cycle that ended in 1990. It was his 1973 novel, *The Tower*, and the money he received for writing it, that put Hollywood stars in his eyes. For the next fifteen years he chased more film deals by writing about group jeopardy and natural disasters (when not writing about Johnny Ortiz): *Power* (atomic reactor, 1974), *Snowbound Six* (blizzard, 1977), *Flood* (water, 1979), *The Big Bridge* (suspension bridge, 1982), *Wildfire* (conflagration, 1985), and *Tsunami* (tidal wave, 1988). None attracted the heat of *The Tower*. Stern died in 2001 in the New Mexico town in which he had set his novels.

Thomas Scortia and Frank M. Robinson wrote five novels over a fourteen year period starting with *The Glass Tower* in 1974. An aerospace worker who wrote on the side, Scortia decided to become a full-time writer when his chosen field of chemistry suffered corporate cutbacks in the early 1970s. Partnering with Frank M. Robinson who, like Scortia, had written science fiction short stories, the team concocted *The Glass Inferno* as their first collaboration. But like all good partnerships, there is a backstory, and this one involves the fractious speculative fiction writer Harlan Ellison.

Scortia and Ellison served together in the Army, although "serving together" is stretching the term. More accurately, according to Ellison, Scortia helped Ellison avoid court martial on one of the three times Ellison wound up in the stockade, probably for insubordination, in the 1950s. Ellison cryptically credits Scortia for this rescue in the preface to one of his books,[91] but notes that the two men drifted apart until shortly before a dying Scortia phoned him in 1986 to mend the rift.

Like his partner, Frank Robinson also had a science background when he started writing: a physics degree from Beloit College. When neither physics nor writing produced a living income, he joined the Navy and, after discharge, went for a journalism degree. Occasional published science fiction pieces and a handful of TV story sales brought him to work at *Rogue*, the Chicago-based men's magazine, in 1959 where Ellison was an editor chafing under the *Rogue*'s scoundrel of a publisher, Bill Hamling.

"Frankie had one of the most infectious laughs of anyone you ever heard," Ellison said. "Frank was an absolute potentate of

____

91 *Angry Candy*, New York: Houghton Mifflin, 1988.

decency. He was the best man I've known, or at least in the top three. He served me in the state of being the older brother I never had."[92] It was Robinson who told Ellison to give up *Rogue* and go back to writing his own material full time. Ellison took the advice and became one of the most successful writers and public personalities of his generation.

Likewise, Robinson flourished not only as a writer but as a gay man who moved to San Francisco to write speeches for Harvey Milk and to become involved in the gay liberation movement. Unlike Stern, Scortia and Robinson kept their hands in Hollywood and sold their 1980 novel, *The Gold Crew*, to NBC which produced it as a 1986 movie called *The Fifth Missile* about a U.S. nuclear submarine crew poisoned by paint fumes and hallucinates that the Russians are attacking. They had sold a previous work, *The Power* (1956),[93] as the basis for the 1968 movie about deadly telekinesis.

The Tower and *The Glass Inferno* are as different as they are alike, and a comparison reveals the challenges in mixing their DNA into a single entity that would reflect the strengths of each and avoid the clumsiness of both.

The Tower begins on the day the 125-story World Tower Building is set to open in lower Manhattan not far from the World Trade Centers at the nonce addresses of 1 WTC and 2 WTC in the city's financial district. It is a proud stainless steel structure fifteen stories taller than 1 WTC and 159 feet higher. Its green-tinted windows challenge the sunrise. Nathan Hale "Nat" Wilson, who represents General Contractor Bertrand McGraw & Company, is rightly proud of the achievement. This is mistake number one, because quite literally the first half of the book details how vulnerable the building is, not to its design flaws, but in the personal flaws of two people involved in its construction.

Unbeknownst to Supervising Architects Caldwell Associates or General Contractor Bertrand McGraw & Company, two dark

---

92 Author interview (unpublished) with Harlan Ellison for *A Lit Fuse: The Provocative Life of Harlan Ellison* (Massachusetts: NESFA Press, 2017). The interview was conducted days after Robinson died in June 2014.

93 Not to be confused with Stern's *Power*.

forces are set against them. The first is the miscreant subcontractor Paul Simmons, McGraw's son-in-law, who has changed the electrical specifications of the building, putting it in jeopardy. The other force is John Connors, a construction worker who had done sheet metal work on the Tower. Connors has had a mental breakdown following the loss of his wife to diabetes and his subsequent firing from his Tower job. In revenge, he sails past the building's guards Mike Shannan and Frank Barnes and commences to plant a small bomb in one of the work rooms. As one hundred and three VIP guests gather in the Tower Room atop the skyrise (which is otherwise unoccupied), Connors is electrocuted, not only killing him ("fried like bacon" is how the firefighter says who discovers his body before vomiting black fluid from the smoke) but knocking the transformers out of commission.

Now corporate politics come into play. Will Giddings, the on-site representative of the owners (World Tower Corporation) wants to call off the party and completely evacuate the building. The company's Grover Frazee staunchly objects saying that the embarrassment would be ruinous. It hardly matters that Mollie Wu, the secretary in Caldwell's office, has her hands on Wilson's original plans that put the lie to Simmons and his counterfeit blueprints. When Wilson sees and compares them, he is horrified.

By now it is too late. Connors's bomb, combined with Simmons's illegal wiring, has sparked fires throughout the structure, disabling the elevators and trapping everyone on the top floor. Sprinklers fail, water boils in the pipes and burst them, and helicopters are unable to land on the tall building because of horrendous crosswinds at that height.

Fire Chief Oliver, aware that there is pressure on Fire Commissioner Timothy O'Reilly Brown, must effect a rescue, but the building's foreboding dynamics stymie him and his crew. Attempts by the trapped guests to escape by the stairs lead them to discover that the doors are blocked by antenna equipment that was left on the other side awaiting to be installed on the roof. Fire fighters rig a breeches buoy between the World

Tower Building and the World Trade Center's north tower but it can transport only one person at a time and will be unable to rescue most of the guests.

As the end approaches, those who cannot escape become philosophical. Some compare their fate to Titanic. Patty (the builder's daughter) and Wilson (the architect) disagree. The Titanic was new; skyscrapers are old and their technology is established. This is about human failure. "Of all the people in the Tower Room," Stern writes, "only a handful understood and accepted not only that catastrophe was in the making, but that it was inevitable. . .one hundred and three persons had drawn numbers. The round trips on the breeches buoy averaged close to one minute. One hour and forty-three minutes, then, would be necessary to evacuate the tower Room. With heat in the building's core already sufficient to distort steel elevator rails, would the Tower Room remain a sanctuary for one hour and forty-three minutes? No So be it."

Four hours and eighteen minutes after the explosion started the fire, it's over. Stern's focus on detail, especially in the early scenes involving Connors's backstory and planting of the explosives, gave a foundation on which to build the rest of the events. He also writes about the tower as if it's a living thing in much the same way that Peter Benchley will begin *Jaws* by writing about the shark. None of this, however, is necessary for a narrative about a burning building; rather, a spark caused by shoddy wiring—a subplot that Stern introduces almost offhandedly—did the job in the movie in a single shot lasting perhaps fifteen seconds. It's as if the mystery writer in Stern was more interested in how things happen than in how those same things affect people.

The Tower provided screenwriter Stirling Silliphant with a corrupt contractor named Simmons, a mayor, a governor, an engineer named Giddings, a builder caught in a public relations bind, and an architect guilty of not paying attention to his own job. Stern's corporate bureaucrat Grover Frazee becomes the movie's PR guy Dan Bigelow, and Nat Wilson's wife Zib Marlowe becomes Doug Roberts's fiancée Susan Thompson. Its philosophical, even clinical, look at personal tragedy worked in print, but a movie requires emotion.

Scortia and Robinson provided more excitement in *The Glass Inferno* as well as more inventiveness for Silliphant to draw upon. In broad strokes, *The Glass Inferno*'s doomed star is The National Curtainwall Company, the bland, formal name of what everyone in the unspecified city calls the Glass House. (And everyone knows that people who live in glass houses shouldn't throw stones.) Merely "one of the tallest" structures in the generic city, its planners were careful to set it on a plaza apart from competing highrises, a decision that will cost them dearly because ladder trucks cannot reach as high on buildings set back from the street. Moreover, the golden skyscraper itself is an accident waiting to happen in that not only does it adhere to only the bare minimum construction codes, the city fire codes themselves are outdated and don't cover skyscrapers such as the sixty-six story Glass House. Its thirty office floors and thirty-six living unit floors are an anomaly; such buildings don't generally combine business and residential. Plus many of its residents have already moved in. This, plus the unauthorized changes in construction materials, sets the fuse for disaster on its day-before-Thanksgiving dedication.

The fire begins spontaneously: a spark from a faulty light switch ignites material in a cluttered storeroom. It could have happened at any time, but it happened late afternoon on an otherwise pleasant day. The architect in *The Glass Inferno* is Craig Barton who asks the building's owner Wyndom Leroux over dinner in the Promenade Room why his specs were altered. Leroux's song and dance about codes and budgets does not mollify Barton.

On one of the business floors the co-owner of a failing home furnishing company starts an arson fire but puts it out when he realizes the harm it will do to his business partner and wife. When he still smells smoke, he is concerned. In the Promenade Room, Barton's and Leroux's dinner is interrupted when they learn that there is a fire on the 17th floor. Barton goes off to investigate while Leroux, his wife Thelma, and Barton's wife Jenny stay and try to eat.

Earlier, the scandal of the substandard construction had come to the attention of a local TV reporter, Jeffrey Quantrell, who obtained incriminating documents from a disgruntled former employee. When the journalist begins his KYS-TV crusade against corruption, he receives threats from all sides. But he also alerts several Glass House residents, including Mrs. Klinger and Lisolette Mueller, to the dangers.

The fire alarm summons Division Chief Mario Infantino who, fortunately, specializes in high-rise fires. Mario is handed control of the fire by Chief Karl Fuchs. Additionally, Barton and Mario have been friends and work together both fighting the fire and uncovering construction flaws. People work their way up to the Promenade Room. Those who are not rescued by helicopters are saved when rooftop water tanks are exploded, dousing the flames. The exterior scenic elevator has its use but ultimately fails. Here, however, Lisolette survives to be reunited with both Harlee Claiborne and her cat. Harry Jernigan, the security man, is a major character. Between him and Quantrell they become a Greek chorus hammering home the dangers of high-rise fires whether caused by corruption or outdated standard building practices.

Combining the books involved more than shuffling pages together. With so much material, it was important to know what to cut and what to keep in no matter how minor it might appear at first reading. In a way it summons the tale of the great sculptor Michelangelo Buonarotti who was asked how he carved his statue of David. "It was easy," he supposedly said but probably didn't, "all I did was remove anything that didn't look like David."

Despite the similarity of plots between *The Tower* and *The Glass Inferno*, the task was one of eliminating backstory and minor characters, which is standard procedure, but also—and here is where Silliphant demonstrated his reputation as a first-class adapter—keeping focused on the characters who are in jeopardy rather than the reasons their lives are on the line. Today's Hollywood lingo calls this "remembering the DNA of the story." As will be noted, its wisdom is revealed in what appears to be an inevitable plot but which was actually the work of someone who knows what looks like David and what doesn't.

Chapter 7: The War to Make *Inferno*

According to legend, it all began over a game of tennis.

Gordon Stulberg, who headed Twentieth Century-Fox in 1973, was relaxing over a weekend tennis game with fellow studio head Ted Ashley who ran Warner Bros. at the time. As moguls will do, they talked shop. Between serves, Ashley and Stulberg discussed properties that each of them had just bought for their respective studios to turn into movies. Ashley was all over *The Tower*, a novel about a skyscraper fire, that they were preparing to spend $4 million shooting. That's funny, Stulberg said, because Fox just bought a novel titled *The Glass Inferno* that's also about a skyscraper fire and we have the same plans, only ours will cost $5 million.

In the decades since then, when $200 million dollars is the common budget for blockbusters and the average studio film costs $65 million,[94] it's well to remember that the average cost of making a movie in the early 1970s was between $750,000 and $3 million.[95] The prospect of two studios spending a combined $9 million on nearly identical films that could cancel each other in the marketplace was intimidating. Yet rather than turn the tennis game into a staring contest, it became a love match; for the first time in modern Hollywood history, two major studios decided to work together to make a single film based on separate properties they each owned. *The Towering Inferno* was born.

But colorful legends have a way of dissolving in the morning dew. *The Towering Inferno* was, indeed, the lovechild of two studios, but

---

94 Gordon Scott review of "Why Movies Cost So Much to Make" by Annie Mueller, *Investopedia*, December 1, 2021, https://www.investopedia.com/financial-edge/0611/why-movies-cost-so-much-to-make.aspx

95 Aljean Harmetz, "How to Pick a Winner," *New York Times*, August 29, 1973

it was legitimate and its actual conception and delivery were far more exciting.

Back when each major studio had a story department and still developed properties (unlike today when they expect producers to do all the work for free), it was routine for publishers to send galleys of their forthcoming releases to film companies. This is what Irwin Allen used to do when he worked for the Orsatti Agency. It's how *The Tower*, by Richard Martin Stern, came to Hollywood in the early months of 1973. Its publisher, the David McKay Company, circulated galleys all around town. Everyone wanted it but not everybody could afford it. When the bidding for the film rights reached $200,000 only three studios were left: Columbia, Fox, and Warners. Columbia dropped out at $250,000. Fox jumped it to $340,000. Then Warner sent them all packing with $390,000 and won. The novel was to be published on October 1, 1973. At the time, Warner was a subsidiary of the Kinney National Company, which owned parking lots but also the Ashley-Famous Talent Agency. Because of anti-trust laws, they had earlier spun off Ashley-Famous and made Ted Ashley head of production.

Two months later, perhaps inspired by McKay's success, Doubleday and Company circulated, not a completed manuscript, but the outline for one called *The Glass Inferno* by Thomas N. Scortia and Frank M. Robinson. It was essentially (and coincidentally) the same story as *The Tower*: fire in a high-rise. It was slated for publication on January 1, 1974. Marvin Birdt, Fox's story editor, raced to New York to buy the film rights on a Friday, and by Monday morning they announced that they owned them for $400,000. Fox's Stulberg made a courtesy call to Warners tipping them off about the sale.[96]

Tennis, anyone?

Stulberg and Ashley had been friends for years. They knew (and had promoted) many of the same people and had risen in the industry as peers. Both were highly respected. And each had

---

96 Aljean Harmetz, "A Funny Thing Happened On the Way to the Fire," *New York Times*, November 18, 1973.

an ace in his hole: Warner had a completed manuscript to begin adapting into a film. But Fox had Irwin Allen.[97]

There was also the issue of budget. Even without a script, it was clear that the burning building picture would cost more than either studio could responsibly spend. Fox was limited by its Board to an $8 million maximum and Stulberg was not confident, even with the recent success of *Poseidon*, that they would accede.[98] Ashley faced a similar challenge from Kinney, so it made sense to play together, but whose ball would they use?

Irwin Allen had immeasurably enriched Fox with his TV series and *The Poseidon Adventure* and was seen as one of the few people in the industry since Cecil B. DeMille who could wrangle a blockbuster. But that didn't mean that he would automatically become the producer.

Allen made the first move and it turned out to be decisive. On July 13, 1973 he and production executive Jere Henshaw invited a cadre of Warners executives to Allen's plush second floor offices in the Fox administration building. Recalled Production Designer William Creber, "The Warners people came over and it was a whole showmanship thing. [Irwin would] dump people out of offices adjacent to him and put up all these storyboards. That was the picture. He would explain to these people what he wanted to do. We had done this bulletin board and it was behind curtains, and he had a button under his chair. We had dummied up a phony poster and they're all kind of dazzled. They sat down and said, 'Irwin, how are you gonna make this picture?' and he goes (buzz), 'Here's our schedule. You see where we are here?' and he goes through the whole thing. They walked away and, when they got back to Warner Bros., there was a telephone call, 'We don't want to be in competition with you. You're gonna kill us'" and handed the ball to Allen.

"They were gonna be equal partners but Warners would take the international, Fox would do domestic, and they would each stay out of the way of the other," recalled David Forbes. "They

---

97 Aljean Harmetz, ibid.
98 Author interview with David M. Forbes, January 17, 2022.

would be fully briefed, but not interfere. The way they had the agreement was that Warners couldn't come in and say they had a better idea to release it on this date and this way, they just went along."

"The idea of joining together and sharing distribution was a relatively new idea," said agent Don Kopaloff, former Avco-Embassy production chief and Stirling Silliphant's agent. "At one time, the studios were very jealous of each other and would never do that. But as costs soared they almost had to do it."[99]

Adds Forbes," Fox was terrified that it was too risky a proposition, but Irwin was negotiating for a little bit more and a little bit more and a little bit more because he saw himself as the master marketer—the great showman, if you will."

In the end, Allen wrung $14 million from both studios and was on his way.[100]

Allen recruited as many of his *Poseidon* collaborators as were available. In addition to production designer William Creber he landed editor Harold F. Kress (who brought in his son, Carl), set decorator Raphael Bretton, costume designer Paul Zastupnevich. special effects expert A.D. Flowers, special visual effects expert L. B. Abbott and matte painter Matt Yuricich, stunt coordinator Paul Stader, cadres of stunt performers and, in post-production, composer John Williams (pre-*Star Wars*), among others.

Locating a building was a matter of geography. The 125-story star of *The Tower* is set in Lower Manhattan. The 66-floor building in *The Glass Inferno* does not specify a city. The story involves a four-alarm fire, so it had to be set in a city that had enough fire departments that could respond. That might have made New York City the perfect place to put the Glass Tower except for one problem: there was no place to put it. Even a cursory examination of the world-famous Manhattan skyline shows—or, rather, doesn't show—any room to plant a 138-story special photographic effect skyscraper.[101] This is why San Francisco was ulti-

---

99 Interviewed in *Hell Under Water, Fire in the Sky*.

100 The initial budget estimate, as reported by Harmetz six months before cameras rolled was $7,000,000.

101 Author conversation with Carl Kress, October 1974.

mately chosen: the skyline had enough space to matte not only the 138-story Glass Tower but the strategically nearby 102-story Peerless Building.

Not surprisingly, Allen had a more Irwin-centric version of the acquisition story. Speaking for a canned public relations interview in 1977, he said, "To begin with, you probably remember that I did a little picture called *The Poseidon Adventure. Poseidon Adventure* started the entire disaster genre and, obviously, we were all looking for other projects of a similar nature. I read a book called *The Tower* and I was fascinated by it and attempted to buy it, but there was no way to get the book because it had already been sold elsewhere. I finally read a book called *The Glass Inferno*. The oddest thing happened—it may have been the first time in the entire history of the publishing business—the two books were exactly the same—same characters, same situations, the same disaster. What happens the night of the celebration of the opening of one of the world's largest buildings, if not *the* tallest building, and there's a terrible calamity in the form of a fire, and the three or four hundred guests who are all invited are all locked off in the penthouse. I attempted to buy *The Glass Tower*[102] (sic). I succeeded in doing so, and then suggested that Warner Bros. and Fox, where I was at the time, join forces and make one single motion picture. Turned out pretty good. As of this moment in time, the picture's already grossed over $200 million worldwide box office which, when you cut it down to the realistic figure, it's $100 million in rentals."[103]

Although Allen had hundreds of scripts under his belt as writer for his TV shows, he knew his skills were no match for the Academy Award®[104]-winning Stirling Silliphant who had made Wendell Mayes's meandering drafts for *The Poseidon Adventure* filmable. He immediately called Silliphant, who was on a Caribbean cruise, and summoned him back to write what had to be a Christmas 1974 release. Losing no time, Silliphant slogged

---

102 For a time during pre-production, *The Towering Inferno* had been titled *The Glass Tower*

103 Canned Irwin Allen PR interview.

104 Silliphant won Best Adapted Screenplay for *In the Heat of the Night* (1967).

through both books and conducted his own research into fire. What he learned would frighten him with each page he wrote and inspire Allen and his team to bring that fear to fruition on the screen.

Chapter 8: Two Goes Into One

"Let me begin by saying that the person in most peril from working on group jeopardy films is the writer," stated Stirling Silliphant, who had survived more than his share of disaster films, having scripted two of the best and also two of the worst.

The then-seventy-five year old Oscar®-winning screenwriter, answering questions by fax from exile in Thailand,[105] was reminiscing about balancing the skill of scripting a disaster picture with the diplomacy of pleasing its all-star cast. The amazing success of *The Poseidon Adventure* didn't insulate Silliphant from a fusillade of egos on *The Towering Inferno*.

"The only ego problem I faced from all the actors on *Towering Inferno*," he recalled with the understatement of distance, "was an occasional (i.e. daily) 'contact' with either Paul Newman or with Steve McQueen or—on blacker days—from both. There was never a problem when they were shooting separate scenes. (Incidentally, I was on the location throughout the filming and therefore, unluckily, in harm's way.) But you put Paul in a scene with Steve and we have an entirely different dynamic at work. I was told, privately and separately, by both gentlemen on one occasion or another, 'Don't let Steve (or Paul) 'blue-eye' me in this scene!' This meant that if you'd written the scene where the punch line comes at the end and the director is likely to cover with a close-up, you'd get Steve socking it across with one of my better lines and laying that cold blue stare right at the camera. Where does that leave Paul? With some kind of vapid reaction shot? No, damn it, now Paul needs a last line. He needs that blue-eyed close-up. It wasn't easy. I think I handled it decently,

---

105 Correspondence interview with Author

because I love Paul and I loved Steve and I just sort of danced around between them and tried to keep all three of us happy."

The jousting began with McQueen's first day on the picture when he insisted that he was having trouble with his dialogue. After several rewrites failed to win the star's approval, Silliphant betrayed frustration. McQueen took him aside and, away from the others, confided that he spoke with a slight lisp and wanted to avoid words with the letter "S" in them. "Well, why didn't you say so?" said Silliphant (himself an "S" man), who easily retooled McQueen's dialogue to make his mouth happy.

Silliphant's biggest problem wasn't sibilance, but balance. With Newman and McQueen counting lines of dialogue and all the stars demanding equal screen time, Silliphant's chief task was developing rich characters with a minimum of pages.

"It's simple math," he said. "Look at the ads Fox and Warners ran: a strip of star photos with shots of Paul Newman and Steve McQueen and Bill Holden and Faye Dunaway and Fred Astaire and Jennifer Jones and Robert Wagner and O. J. Simpson and Richard Chamberlain, etc. etc., each labeled 'the fireman,' 'the architect,' 'the builder,' 'the contractor', etc., etc. actually labeling the stereotype in advance for the potential viewer.

"Okay, we had seven major narrative thrusts to fold in—seven major separate personal relationships to be introduced, developed, strained, then resolved—along with their interaction with another group—Holden with Chamberlain, Holden with his daughter, Holden with Newman, Holden with McQueen—seven of the bloody things—and then the eighth character—the FIRE itself (which, while I wrote, I gave a name to—MY secret—but my favorite character in the script). I determined to let the fire WIN—make it the hero—but I always knew that, in the end, the good guys—the architect and the fireman—would have to triumph.

"That's only the beginning of your problems," he continued. "You have to deal with the logistics of the physical action and this becomes a matter of charting, not writing. If something blows up on the fifty-seventh floor and in the scene before that you had Paul Newman down on the thirty-second floor and the elevators can't be used, how are you going to get him up there? Simple, let him use the stairway. What if the stairway collapses on his way up? Okay, we need a scene about that. So before you can get the man up there to do his few pages, you now have to create a new scene out of the mechanical motivations of the action. Jesus, guys, where did we leave Steve McQueen in his last scene before we had to cut away to Fred Astaire looking for Jennifer Jones's cat?"[106]

Novelists can finesse far more than screenwriters; they have pages and pages with which to tweak narrative points. Screenwriters must nail every action because it's going to be seen, no fudging allowed. To help Silliphant keep track of who was where, Irwin Allen provided him with models and floor plans by which he could track the action. Then, of course, there were two novels with a collective length of over seven hundred pages to draw from, right?[107]

Well, sort of. Silliphant long maintained that, although he was hired to combine both *The Tower* and *The Glass Inferno* into a single script, he only ever read one of them and he forgot which one it was. Turns out he was being glib; the truth lies in a thirty-seven page document dated August 22-23, 1973 that was discovered among Silliphant's personal papers. It contains a massive amount of research about high rise building fires. In the notes he specifically cites only *The Glass Inferno* by title, but his script reveals that he culled characters and situations from both. At one point he also discloses that, for a while, the working title of the film was *The Glass Tower*.

Silliphant was a research wonk who would stuff his brain with data until it exploded onto paper. On August 9, 1973 he began his research with a location survey to the Occidental Tower (336 Occidental Boulevard), Los Angeles' tallest structure. He had lunch with building manager Ewing and chief engineer Campbell in the thirty-two story structure's Tower Restaurant. There he

---

106   Author correspondence interview with Silliphant, op cit.
107   Hardcover editions of *The Tower* (343) and *The Glass Inferno* (374).

leaned, firsthand, the challenges of building and operating such a structure. On another trip he had lunch with a fire official who, after touring that city's highest building, insisted on eating in a basement restaurant and sitting under the sprinkler system.

Silliphant visited six cities and among his shocking discoveries (circa 1974) were:

- Most fire-fighting equipment cannot reach above the thirteenth-story level of a building; aerial fire ladders only reach the eighth floor; hoses can only throw water 500 feet;
- Fire-safety requirements have not kept pace with rapidly changing building designs;
- Some elevator call buttons are activated by the heat of the finger that presses them, causing elevators to automatically home to the fire floor, open up, and incinerate their passengers;
- Central air conditioning is the perfect way to spread smoke and fire, and the gap between ceilings and floors is a space for fumes to gather and ignite;
- Modern office furniture and carpeting made of plastic and foam release toxic gasses when burned;
- Some fire-resistant coatings may protect furniture and clothing but they emit carbon monoxide (CO) in lieu of permitting combustion of the material they're applied to. CO kills rapidly. As little as one-tenth of one percent in the air will cause severe headache and nausea in one hour, a coma in two hours, and death in four;
- As window glass breaks, fresh air rushes in to create a flame flash;
- A stairway will discharge about ninety people per minute which means that only ninety people can enter the stairway per minute once the stairway has been filled;
- Today we find we have built air-conditioned boxes. We frequently hang panel walls from the floor deck, leaving open spaces between the wall and the deck. We punch the entire system full of holes to contain air-conditioning ducts,

utility cables, and other equipment. In place of heavy mass concrete and masonry, which tend to absorb a great deal of the heat of a fire, we use highly effective insulating materials which tend to bottle the heat of the fire. On top of this we install fixed windows, which prohibit emergency venting. Fire attack in high-rise buildings today is extremely difficult, dangerous, and, some say, nearly impossible;

- Bottom line: Who started this fire? Who didn't? The public, who is indifferent. The building owner who. . .The Fire commissioners who. . .The product designers who give little thought to possible toxic or fire-aggravating effects should their products become involved in fire.[108]

Armed—or, more likely, terrified—by this information, Silliphant began constructing his script. And *constructing* was the right word. "Now, you have a script of 130 pages," he said. "You have eight major story-character blocks. Eight goes into 130 around sixteen-plus times. So you know, going in, that you can only put Holden on sixteen pages of the movie in terms of foreground action or any kind of meaningful dialogue unless you unbalance everything and give him twenty-two pages and cut Chamberlain to ten, etc., etc., etc. Yes, I call that FRUSTRATING because what you are not doing is writing. What you are doing is juggling."

His writing methods reflected decades of experience. He used a Selectric II typewriter[109] and preferred yellow paper ("easier on the eyes," he told interviewer William Froug).[110] He divided the scenes from his prose treatment into separate pages and kept them in a loose-leaf notebook, taking out one scene summary at a time and expanding it into script pages, then putting it back in. He was incredibly fast, believing that it shouldn't take any longer to write a script than it will take to film it. For the aver-

---

108 Stirling Silliphant, unpublished notes August 22-23, 1973, the Estate of Stirling Silliphant.

109 The Selectric II with the "golf ball" and adhesive correction tape had been introduced in March 1973 and you can bet Silliphant was among of the first to buy one.

110 William Froug, *The Screenwriter Looks at the Screenwriter* (Mew York: Macmillan, 1972.

age film, this meant ten to twelve weeks.[111] *The Towering Inferno* took longer, but then so was its script."[112]

The master of creating scenes that both defined character and moved the story forward, Silliphant lost no time delineating memorable first appearances for his superstar cast. Stars know they're in good hands when they read a script and see a noteworthy entrance, and Silliphant did not disappoint. Moreover, what's significant is not only that the stars are seen to advantage but that their actions in their first scenes deftly describe their characters and advance the plot.

In order of appearance (elapsed screen time shown in parentheses):

Paul Newman (0:03:58): Riding in a helicopter across rural California, then swooping toward the skyline which is dominated by his brand new building, and he's smiling all the way.

William Holden (0:04:41): steps onto roof heliport and greets Newman emerging from chopper, then tries to persuade him to continue designing buildings for him, so we know he's a developer.

Faye Dunaway (0:08:04): Revealed as she stands after sitting in a deep chair in Newman's office and kissing him hello, then telling him she has a newspaper job offer that may separate them.

Fred Astaire (0:09:08): Gets out of a taxi and charmingly cheats the driver out of a tip.

Jennifer Jones: (0:10:48): Revealed finishing art lessons with two children, showing concern as she wipes the little girl's hands clean of paint.

The Fire (0:12:43): Begins as sparks fly from a supply room fuse box onto paper and rags and sets them ablaze.

O.J. Simpson (0:12:48): Surveys the work his security team is doing in their command headquarters, then notices an anomaly in the alarm system.

---

111 Nat Segaloff, "Stirling Silliphant: The Finger of God" (*Backstory 3*, Patrick McGilligan, ed., California: University of California Press, 1997; copyright transferred 2001; expanded into *Stirling Silliphant: The Fingers of God* (Albany, Georgia: BearManor Media, 2013)

112 Typical feature screenplays run 97 to 110 pages. *The Towering Inferno* was 156.

Robert Wagner (0:16:48): Enters William Holden's office carrying the gold scissors to be used in that night's dedication. (He was originally introduced in an earlier, deleted scene going over the dedication program with his PR staff.)

Susan Blakely (0:19:12): Answers the door of her mansion to admit Paul Newman. They discuss possible whereabouts of her errant husband.

Richard Chamberlain (0:20:12): Comes home and immediately ducks Newman's accusation that he cut corners on the building construction.

Robert Vaughn (0:26:23): Cuts through the crowd gathered in the street and is announced by the event emcee to make a speech about the importance of this event.

Susan Flannery (0:30:28): The camera finds her as she is called into Robert Wagner's office to take a letter, but actually to have an assignation. (She also appeared in a now-deleted scene welcoming the jeweler with the gold scissors that will be used to cut the dedication ribbon.)

Steve McQueen (0:43:24): Pulls up in the Chief's car, squeals to a stop, gets out, and not only issues orders, he grills Newman about why systems aren't working, explaining for the audience what they are up against. In the script, O'Hallorhan had earlier domestic scenes with his family but those do not appear in the final edit. McQueen is therefore the last to be introduced, but by then all the expository elements have been established and they all point to him as the one who will resolve everything.

Silliphant played mix-and-match with the characters in developing their dramatic stories: Fred Astaire romancing Jennifer Jones to sell her his worthless stock certificates; William Holden conspiring with Faye Dunaway to keep Paul Newman from quitting; Richard Chamberlain blaming his corruption on Holden's pressure to come in on budget; Robert Vaughn, the senator running the urban renewal committee, being compromised by developer Holden; Susan Flannery and Robert Wagner's affair about to go up in flames; and Faye Dunaway commiserating with Susan Blakely about the men in their lives. The only character who remains merely functional and does his recue job is O.J. Simpson.

When McQueen arrives, of course, what could have become a predictable clash with Newman surprisingly becomes a collaboration to fight the fire which is, after all, the common enemy. Notably, McQueen doesn't care why the wiring is substandard, the sprinklers aren't operational, or the exhaust system has failed. His concern is solely and resolutely putting out the fire and saving lives.

For all his talk of "blue eye" scenes, Silliphant avoids wise-cracks or lines that signal a "cut to." Director John Guillermin, producer/action director Irwin Allen, and editors Karl and Harold F. Kress are able to cut from one climax to the next motivated by the action rather than a dialogue cue. This is a result of the many locations on which Silliphant has set his action; if one scene becomes boring, the film cuts to another one. In keeping so many plates spinning on sticks, Silliphant has effectively directed the film on paper despite the dramatic skills of Guillermin and the action expertise of Allen.

By the time Silliphant wrote *The Towering Inferno* he had gone through personal changes that included several marriages, a murdered son, an estranged daughter, and a spiritual awakening. In the late 1960s, he embraced Buddhism ("within," he explained, "the limits of a still-remaining pragmatic Western orientation").[113] He began studying both the martial arts and Eastern beliefs with Bruce Lee. He kept much of what he had absorbed in his mind as he wrote the screenplay for *The Towering Inferno*, particularly the lessons Man can learn from Nature. He cited aphorisms such as, "We are vigilant, but we are not vigilantes," "I will not question your sincerity, I will only question the extent of it," and "After the bird has flown, what do you do with the cage?" He also wrestled with guilt, both religious and ethical, writing, "Do I have guilt feelings? Of course I have guilt feelings. Anybody brought up under the Judeo-Christian ethic who doesn't have guilt feelings is not only insensitive, he's a goddamned liar." The thread of

---

113 Correspondence with the author for "The Finger of God," op cit.

guilt, actual or existential, runs through the entirety of *The Towering Inferno* and affects nearly every character. In a way, this is what makes the film more moving to an audience than a simple action picture, for it makes each viewer question the value that each of them places on his, her, their, or others' lives.

Despite these challenges, Silliphant concluded, "*The Towering Inferno* did emerge as a powerful and engrossing film, I have to admit, despite all my assaults against having my writing driven by forces beyond my control. I believe this happened because we really took after the shoddy builders, the contractors who gamble with human lives to save a buck—so there was underneath all the never-ending action—and despite the superficiality of the characters, a deeper dynamic, a humanistic point which lifted the film an inch or two above its own genre. Naturally, I was astonished when it was nominated for an Academy Award® as one of the five best movies of the season. There was no way it could ever win, but at least we all got to put on our tuxedos and eat the standard chicken dinner at one of the big-time hotels."

The result of Silliphant's writing and juggling act was the delivery of a 156-page, 604-scene "Second Revised Final" shooting script dated March 29, 1974. It would, as anticipated, be changed throughout the course of the fourteen-weeks of principal photography which began on May 8, 1974. Meanwhile, it was essential for final budgeting and scheduling and so, in flux or not, preproduction picked up.

Chapter 8 Sidebar: Script Revisions

Lest it be thought that screenplays are a one-draft thing, here is a list of the revisions that Stirling Silliphant made in the course of pre-production and production.[114] The reasons for rewrites are numerous: improving a scene, an actor's demands, budget constraints, the addition of new story elements, a producer's whim, or even his or her own better idea. All of these weighed upon Silliphant—who was one of the most agreeable and fastest writers in the business—with the following results.

It also didn't hurt that he was paid for every one of them:

Step outlines: A step-outline is a beat sheet of each scene in the proposed film written as a separate capsule description of what happens. A screen treatment is a prose narrative of the proposed film, rich in detail and dialogue, that looks and reads like a novella. An important feature is that it is told in the present tense to describe what is happening on the screen. Writing in the present tense is a helpful discipline in film. It doesn't allow interior thought ("he felt," "she wanted") which is something that cannot work in the third-person medium of film, which always operates in time-present. Silliphant wrote ten step outlines and screen treatments between August 15, 1973 and August 23, 1973. After the final treatment was approved, he began the script itself of which there are thirteen drafts in his collection reflecting changes within but not starting over from scratch:

1. September 26, 1973: First draft screenplay based on previous treatments
2. October 19, 1973: Revisions to September 26 screenplay. Notation "Pink."[115]

---

114   Stirling Silliphant papers, UCLA Performing Arts Special Collections.
115   "Pink" refers to the color paper onto which the script was printed. Each revision has its own color. The first draft is on white, and after that: 2-Blue, 3-Pink, 4-Yellow, 5-Green, 6-Goldenrod, 7-buff,

3. October 15, 1973: Revised Brown
4. November 5, 1973: rewrite of October 26 pink sheets
5. November 16, 1973: Yellow
6. November 30, 1973: Revised second draft pages
7. December 7, 1973: Revised second draft]
8. December 12, 1973: Revisions
9. January 11, 1974: "Shooting final"[116]
10. January 30, 1974: Major rewrite with different opening scene, changed character relationships, new set pieces, and full story.
11. February 15, 1974: Second revised shooting final
12. March 29, 1974: Third revised shooting final. The script itself reads "Second revised," but Silliphant's notes say "Third revised."
13. April 18, 1974: Fourth revised shooting final.[117]

8-Salmon, 9-Cherry, 10-Second Blue, 11-Second Pink (etc.). The result is what's called a "rainbow script." As archived, however, this spectrum was either abandoned or never used.

116 "Shooting final" is generally considered wishful thinking.

117 Although the first day of principal photography was May 8, 1974, Silliphant would continue, as noted, to make revisions throughout production.

Chapter 9: Casting a Disaster

How can two stars have first billing? That was the diplomatic quandary faced by Irwin Allen when he approached Paul Newman and Steve McQueen to star in *The Towering Inferno*. Newman and McQueen, both of them A-list box office attractions, were no strangers to working together, albeit behind the scenes. They were partners in First Artists, a production company formed in 1969 with goading from their Creative Artists Agency agents Freddie Fields and David Begelman. Not unlike United Artists, upon whose founding in 1919 by Douglas Fairbanks, Mary Pickford, Charlie Chaplin, and D.W. Griffith Hollywood wags joked, "the lunatics have taken over the asylum," First Artists was designed to give control to its above-the-title partners of the films in which they appeared. In addition to McQueen and Newman, the company included Barbra Streisand, Dustin Hoffman, and Sidney Poitier.[118]

Stars mingling together off-screen is one thing, but when they share the screen, friendship goes by the boards.[119] With agents Fields and Begelman involved, and with Irwin Allen pushing Warner Bros. (Ted Ashley and John Calley) and Twentieth Century-Fox (Gordon Stulberg and Alan Ladd, Jr.) to sign these mega-stars, offers were extended to Steve McQueen to play the architect and to Paul Newman to play the fire chief.

"Irwin wanted Steve to play the architect," said Sheila Mathews (who would marry Irwin Allen three months after the

---

118   First Artists dissolved in 1980 for a variety of reasons. Their eclectic fare (both of subjects and profitability) included such titles as *Straight Time*, *Agatha*, *Up the Sandbox*, *Pocket Money*, *An Enemy of the People*, *A Star is Born*, *Uptown Saturday Night*, *The Getaway*, and *The Main Event*.

119   An amusing example of billing was Spencer Tracy and Katharine Hepburn in *Adam's Rib*. When co-writer Garson Kanin suggested that Hepburn go first, Tracy responded, "This is a movie, not a lifeboat."

film came out) and Steve read the script and he said, 'I don't like to talk that much.'"[120]

The idea did seem backward. McQueen's appeal has always been as an action hero (his portrayal of the ivy league bank thief mastermind in 1968's *The Thomas Crown Affair* was seen as a stretch) while Newman's image was more contemplative. The first to respond was McQueen who, to the surprise of some, wanted to play the fire chief. This was ascribed at the time to the star's penchant for action roles and because he wanted to ride fire trucks.

Stunt performer Loren James, who often served as McQueen's stand-in, agrees. "I think he wanted to play the fireman because it was an action thing and it was the knowledge of knowing what to do and how to do it rather than being an architect with a coat and tie and that sort of thing."

Robert Vaughn, who co-starred with McQueen in *The Magnificent Seven* in 1960, said, "Steve had an enormous interest in police work and fire work before the film, and when he was told he was going to play a fire captain he was delighted because he could get to work with fire engines and wear a fireman's costume. He had a kind of a child-like quality about him in terms of uniforms and things." But then he added, "Steve was exceedingly paranoid about everything, so if he could control his situation on a film in terms of billing or in terms of salary and things, he would be the first one to speak up, whereas Paul would be in the background probably feeling the same way, but he wouldn't be paranoid, he'd just say, "talk to my agent, talk to my lawyer, talk to my manager.""[121]

The truth is more involved. When McQueen, canny as ever about his persona, was approached to play the architect, it was

---

120 This desire for terseness would conflict with McQueen's insistence on having the same number of lines of dialogue as Newman and was made worse with the removal of early domestic scenes involving his character. This resulted in his entering the film at the forty-six minute point after many of Newman's line allotment had been used on exposition. (Pretty cagey, Steve)

121 Mathews, James, and Vaughn comments from *Hell Under Water, Fire in the Sky*, Directed by Andrew Abbott, Nobles Gate, Ltd. 2003

thought that Ernest Borgnine, late of *Poseidon*, would play the fire chief. This meant that, star-wise, the weight of the film would rest solely on McQueen's shoulders. Seeking to add depth to the architect's role, he at first demanded that a backstory be added to "Craig Barton" explaining that he had been absent from the final phase of building construction because he was supervising "The Idaho Project," an environmentally conscious real estate development in another state. This would explain (as it does when Paul Newman inherited the role) why he wants to ditch skyscrapers and go back to forests. Not only that, an earlier script draft had Barton's girlfriend having an affair with Roger Simmons for no particular reason. McQueen bailed on that storyline and chose to play the fire chief, suggesting his First Artists partner Paul Newman for the architect.

More insightfully, McQueen may have chosen to play O'Hallorhan for a much wiser, more subtle reason: the fire chief is the only major character in the story who is without guilt.[122] Everyone else—from Duncan the builder to his son-in-law the contractor to the collaborating politicians and, yes, even the architect who failed to bird-dog the final stages of construction—is, to some degree, responsible for the fire. McQueen was widely known for having a keen sense of self-preservation, and this proves it.

So did Paul Newman, but in a different way: both he and McQueen demanded $1 million salary plus ten percent of the gross (not net) and got it.[123]

Then there arose the problem of billing.

"The Newman-McQueen thing was Who was first and who was higher?" explained David Forbes, who directed *Inferno*'s marketing program. "Irwin sat in the middle of the negotiations, and it's not normal—or at least it wasn't then—for the producer to be doing those deals, and he ended up making one actor (McQueen)

---

122 Author's conversation with Scott Newman, October 1974.

123 Some sources say 7.5 percent. Additionally, each man was obligated to make another picture for Allen. This would have disastrous results six years later when Newman made *When Time Ran Out* (q.v.). If McQueen indeed had a similar obligation, he and Allen never worked together again.

first so that his name would be up on the screen first, and the other actor (Newman) higher, even though his name was on the other side of the screen. So one could say, 'I'm higher' and the other could say 'I'm first.'"[124] This contrivance continues even in the end cast list, after which the costars are listed in order of appearance and everyone else in no discernable order.[125]

Billing for the studios was simpler: Twentieth Century-Fox got first billing in North America where they handled distribution and Warner Bros. got first billing internationally where distribution was their responsibility. (And you can bet that there wasn't going to be any "Hollywood bookkeeping" either way in that deal.)

At the time, an all-star cast like this was an anomaly. Big-budget films usually had one top male star, one top female star, and character actors or lesser stars in supporting roles. Hollywood hadn't seen Allen's kind of stellar alchemy since MGM put most of their biggest names into *Grand Hotel* and *Dinner at Eight* in the early 1930s.

To Irwin Allen, it made sense. "When you insure your motion picture with the best that money can buy," he reasoned, "when you sprinkle it with stars like the caliber of Steve McQueen and Paul Newman and William Holden and Faye Dunaway and Fred Astaire and Jennifer Jones and Robert Vaughn and Bob Wagner and O.J. Simpson, etc., etc., you run less of a risk, although it is [more] risky spending fifteen million than you do spending two, three, or even four million."[126]

While stars like McQueen and Newman were tough negotiators, others were pushovers. "I didn't know anything about the script," said Susan Blakely, who played William Holden's ill-married daughter, Patty. "I hadn't read the script. But when my agent

---

124 David Forbes interviewed in *Hell Under Water, Fire in the Sky*, Directed by Andrew Abbott, Nobles Gate, Ltd. 2003

125 McQueen had originally been romanced to play the Sundance Kid opposite Newman in *Butch Cassidy and the Sundance Kid* in 1969. This would have resulted in a similar billing issue. When he passed on the project, the role was offered to Robert Redford who did not have Newman's stature at the time, although he attained it once the film became a hit.

126 Promotional interview clip for *The Towering Inferno*, Twentieth Century-Fox, 1974.

told me that it was Paul Newman and Steve McQueen and Bill Holden and Fred Astaire I said, 'I don't have to read it; of course I'll do it.' And when I read it, I was actually a little surprised that all these people were doing that movie because it was a genre I didn't know about, I just didn't get that kind of thing.[127]

Blakely had just one scene alone with Newman: when he comes to her house looking for her wayward husband. John Guillermin directed dramatic scenes such as this. "That was the only scene I had with Paul Newman," Blakely remembered. "The funny part was before I go to the door. I'd hear John say, 'Action.' Then I'd go to the door and every time I answered it, I wanted to say, 'Oh My God! Paul Newman!' That's how excited I was to work with Paul Newman."[128]

Casting wasn't as easy as choosing dinner from an ala carte menu. Olivia de Havilland was first offered the role that went to Jennifer Jones. Known for such prestigious films as *The Snake Pit* (1948), *The Heiress* (1949), and, of course, *Gone with the Wind* (1939), the elegant de Havilland was also no stranger to the fate that befalls older actresses in Hollywood with a string of popcorn fare such as *Lady in a Cage, Hush. . .Hush Sweet Charlotte* (both 1964), and TV's *The Screaming Woman* (1972). For whatever the reason was that she passed on *Inferno*, it wasn't because she didn't like disaster pictures; three years later she made *Airport '77*. For a moment there was even talk of asking Ginger Rogers to play Lisolette, raising the possibility of reuniting her with Fred Astaire. The mind reels. In any event, the role went to Jones.

In the end, the casting magic worked. "Assembling the kind of cast he assembled for *Towering Inferno*, in particular," appraised marketer David Forbes, "made him feel like he achieved even greater success, or greater accomplishment than he had with *Poseidon Adventure* or anything that had preceded that."[129]

---

127 Interviewed in *Hell Under Water, Fire in the Sky,* op cit.
128 Author interview with Susan Blakely, July 13, 2022.
129 ibid

Producer (and sometimes director and writer) Irwin Allen, the "Master of disaster" and an unashamed movie lover. (credit: Photofest)

"The Life of an American Fireman" may be the movies' first storytelling film. Shot and edited by Edwin S. Porter for the Thomas Edison Company in 1902, it shows a fireman dreaming of a family; someone pulling the alarm box; A daring rescue; and firemen fighting the flames.

Noah's Ark (1928) was an early disaster film involving water which, according to some sources, injured and took the lives of several extras. Michael Curtiz directed.

In One Million B.C. (1940), Hal Roach Sr., Hal Roach, Jr. and perhaps D. W. Griffith used miniatures to create an erupting volcano and oatmeal for its lava.

The aftermath of the 1906 San Francisco Earthquake was more terrible than any disaster movie. (Wiki Commons photo by George R. Lawrence)

The Towering Inferno was a blend of two simultaneously, coincidentally published books about high-rise fires: The Tower by Richard Martin Stern and The Glass Inferno by Thomas N. Scortia and Frank Robinson.

After decades of movies and TV, The Poseidon Adventure (1972) was Allen's first box office smash. Showing off their Oscars® during a break in filming are (L-R): Jack Albertson (for The Subject Was Roses, 1969), Red Buttons (for Sayonara, 1957) Ronald Neame, Gene Hackman (who would win for The French Connection, 1971, during shooting), Shelley Winters (The Diary of Anne Frank, 1959, and A Patch of Blue, 1965), and Ernest Borgnine (Marty, 1955). Winters would be nominated for an Oscar for Poseidon. (Photo credit: Wiki Commons by Bruce H. Cox, Los Angeles Times)

Paul Newman and Steve McQueen take a break from counting each other's lines.

Screenwriter Stirling Silliphant was tasked with combing two books into one coherent script. For years he maintained that he'd only read one of them and has forgotten which one it was. In fact, he made meticulous notes, as documents demonstrate that were discovered for this book.

This "One Happy Family" group photo—a Hollywood tradition on multi-star films—was distributed to publicists to place in newspapers. Days later the studio sent an urgent fax not to use it. The reason? It doesn't contain Susan Flannery and Susan Blakely. Susan Blakely was a recent addition to the cast, replacing another actress who had to drop out for undisclosed reasons. A Telex to field publicists killed the photo (Author's collection).

Irwin Allen and Paul Newman prepare for an action sequence, which Allen directed.

Paul Stader was Stunt Coordinator on Inferno and other Irwin Allen productions.

Irwin Allen was right at home behind a bullhorn — that is, when he wasn't firing guns to get his actors' attentions.

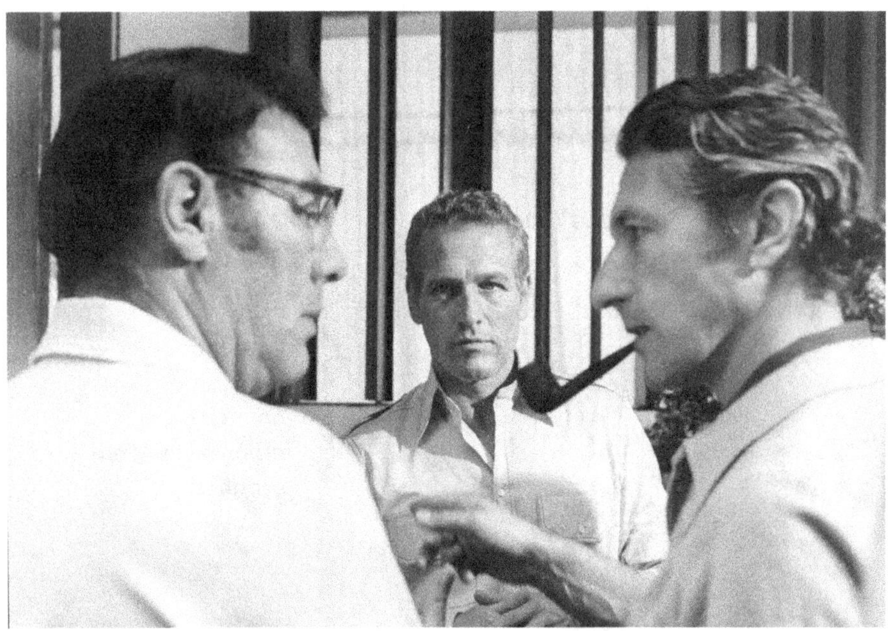

Irwin Allen, Paul Newman, and John Guillermin (who directed the dramatic scenes) have a confab. (credit: Photofest).

Irwin Allen (R) attends a sneak preview of The Towering Inferno *at the Showcase Cinema, Hartford, Connecticut to gauge audience reaction. The author, who was then a publicist on the film, is the one in the background needing a haircut. (Author's collection)*

The San Francisco Skyline as it is (Wiki Commons photo by Daniel Ramirez) and as it appears in The Towering Inferno. *San Francisco was chosen as the setting because, among other reasons, its skyline had room to matte in two high rises.*

The logo and splash poster for The Towering Inferno. *Subsequent posters would feature thumbnails of the stars identified not by their names but by their roles: "the architect," "the security guard," etc.*

Scott Newman, son of Paul Newman, appeared as a nervous firefighter.

When The Towering Inferno *hit the home screen it was a major viewing event.*

Chapter 10: Lighting the Match

The Towering Inferno hit the ground flaming on May 8, 1974 with a mandate to open in theatres on December 14, seven months hence. Only meticulous planning by Irwin Allen and his team could make that possible, and they had been on the job even before Fox's and Warner's business nuptials.

The spacious lobby of the San Francisco Hyatt Regency hotel, recently opened at 5 Embarcadero, with its glass sightseeing elevators, doubled for the lobby of the Glass Tower.[130] The company shot for three weeks in the City by the Bay, much of it at night. The exterior of the movie's skyscraper was the base and plaza of the Bank of America World Headquarters at 555 California Street in Los Angeles.[131] Matte paintings by Matthew Yuricich added to its apparent height. Two scale replicas of the building were created: a sixty-foot model of five floors and a complete 138-floor model rising seventy feet at one-half inch/foot scale. (It was seventy feet because that was how far a camera crane could then extend.) A shorter model of the Peerless building was created and, paired with the seventy-foot model, was matted (superimposed) onto the San Francisco skyline.[132] They were not cheap:

> $50,000 for the 1.8 scale exterior for shots involving actors;

---

130 Later reused by Mel Brooks for *High Anxiety* (1977).

131 The BofA didn't want their building identified at the time. This is the same build from whose rooftop Scorpio (Andy Robinson) shot his first victim in *Dirty Harry* (1971).

132 At this writing the tallest actual structure in San Francisco is the 61-story, 1,079-foot Salesforce Tower.

$35,000 for 1.24 scale seen in the same frame as the
Peerless Building;
$16,000 for miniatures of the water storage tanks to
blow up;
$33,000 for interior miniatures;
$18,000 for lighting and physical effects including fuel
feeds.

The advantage of having such large miniatures was that (as noted earlier) the fire and water, when photographed at 48, 72, and sometimes 96 frames per second in such a huge structure, looked acceptably realistic. Combined with A. D. Flowers' explosions, the ping of windows shattering, and the whoosh of flames shooting from the façade, all of it against a pitch black night sky on the Fox ranch, the aggregate effect was more than acceptable.[133]

From blueprints created by production illustrator Joseph Musso, a five-floor stretch of the building exterior was constructed on the Fox Ranch in Malibu. This was used for action that was set anywhere at the front of the building. A double for the base of the building and its first three floors was built on the Fox backlot in what later became Century City.[134] Equipment rooms in the tower were shot in the air conditioning floor of a Century City hospital.

The film used fifty-seven sets[135] that were built on eight soundstages. Seven of them were completely enclosed to contain the fire effects. Only eight were left standing by the end.

---

133 Special visual effects cinematographer L.B. Abbott could have used the trick that Douglas Trumbull perfected on *Blade Runner* and *Close Encounters of the Third Kind* of filling the air with oil mist to diffuse the sharp-edged photography into something that more closely resembled seeing objects at a distance.

134 Charles Loring, "*The Towering Inferno* and How It Was Filmed," *American Cinematographer* magazine, February 1975.

135 As noted earlier, the author was New England publicity representative for *The Towering Inferno*. One Monday he arrived at Fox's business office in Boston's Park Square Building to discover that the floor had been covered during the weekend with strange chartreuse-colored carpeting. Only when he saw the film and noticed that the Promenade Room set had the same carpeting did he realize that the studio had refurbished its office at Irwin Allen's expense, I always wondered what Warner Bros. got out of it.

The production team was divided into four units:

1. Dramatic scenes directed by John Guillermin and photographed by Fred J. Koenekamp, A.S.C.;
2. Action unit directed by Irwin Allen and photographed by Joseph Biroc, A.S.C.;
3. Special Effects unit coordinated by L.B. (Lenwood Ballard) "Bill" Abbott (who came out of retirement to work on the film);
4. Aerial unit under the direction of Jim Freeman of MacGillivray/Freeman Films.

"It was an involved picture in that it had a number of units," Irwin Allen explained for a studio publicity interview. "It had the special effects unit, there was the action unit, there was the principal photography unit. Each of these had to be designed so that, one, they could stand up by themselves, and, two, that they could be properly blended with one another. I looked for the best of the effects people and Bill Abbott, who's been with me for almost twenty years, and has won, oh, I dunno, eight Academy Awards® for special effects, was my number one choice because we knew there were gonna be an unusual amount of effects. I chose John Guillermin to be the director to work with me because of the work that John had done in the past.[136] My art director (sic) was Bill Creber who had done a magnificent job on *The Poseidon Adventure*. Bill Creber, along with Bill Abbott and a number of other people who went with me on *Towering Inferno*, were chosen because of the great work they did there. I picked myself to not only be the producer but to do the so-called 'action unit' directing. It's something I particularly enjoy and I guess I must be pretty good, otherwise they wouldn't have allowed me to do it. We all worked pretty well together; the end result was *The Towering Inferno*."

---

136 Allen is making the best of it. In truth, he yearned to direct the entire film but, despite his having an Oscar® and thirteen TV and feature directing credits by then, including for Fox, the studio insisted on Guillermin. Nevertheless, Allen's action (second unit) scenes comprise some forty-five percent of the finished picture.

The sets, in particular the 135th-floor Promenade Room, were designed to burn. In addition to the expected carpets, draperies, furniture, and fixtures, they had hidden pipes through which kerosene could be fed and quickly shut off to create fire effects. "When [Bill Holden and I] walked into the soundstage on the first day we were terribly impressed with the scale," said Robert Vaughn. "It seemed to have been built directly to scale as would a real ballroom. And, of course, all the fire stuff that went on in the ballroom was fascinating to watch. It was a picture where we all loved watching the special effects where we were involved because they were very carefully organized in terms of [not] hurting anyone or causing any real disasters of any kind. And I don't think anyone was hurt on the film as far as I know."[137]

It was a tricky shoot to schedule. All the scenes shot on pristine sets had to be finished before the sets could be burned. Moreover, directors Guillermin and Allen—or, more precisely, their cinematographers—had to make sure that their footage, shot separately, could be intercut. Similarly, costume designer Paul Zastupnevich had to make two costumes for each of the main characters: one that was kept in perfect shape and another that could be increasingly distressed as the plot thickened. Even though the sets couldn't go back and forth, the actors could.

For obvious reasons, heat was a constant bane. There were as many as thirty people from the Los Angeles, San Francisco, and Fox studio fire departments during the filming of fire scenes. Battalion Chief Jack Cavello of the San Francisco Fire Department was assigned as technical advisor; Battalion Chief Pete Lucarelli of the Los Angeles Fire Department performed a similar role, and when the stars were involved with fire, each of them had a fire fighter as guard. All the sets were closed off to prevent the spread of flames, and no fire scene could last more than thirty seconds because the sprinkler system would go off.

---

137 Interviewed in *Hell Under Water, Fire in the Sky*. According to reports, there was one injury during production: a technical advisor cut his finger on a piece of glass.

In that regard, production designer William Creber recalled, "We were talking about the temperature in the sound stage tripping the sprinklers because all the stages had sprinklers. So I said, 'Well, during the filming, why don't we just shut the valves off and we won't have a problem?' and [technical advisor Ed] Conlon said, 'Tell you what: shutting off a sprinkler system in a building with the express purpose of lighting a fire is called arson.' So we had a fireman up there with a thermometer and he would walk around and when the temperature up in the permanents got to a point where it would set the sprinklers off, he would shut the company down. It started out that we had twenty minutes to film and it got down to five, it got so hot."[138]

"Unlike working with water," explained Irwin Allen, "water will stand still in a big bathtub if you ask it to until you're ready for the next shot. But once you light that match, you've got to be ready to have all eight cameras grinding at one time because fire waits for no man. As a result of it, we did a lot of burning. Fire, obviously, is terribly dangerous, even more so than water. Happily, despite the fact that we successfully burned down the world's tallest building for motion picture purposes, we wound up with no fatalities, thank God, and very few cuts and bruises."[139]

The fire had to be not only controlled but, to whatever extent possible, directed. Propane was chosen because "it's heavier than air," explained pyrotechnics expert Thane Morris, "so you can oft-times walk propane across the floor and then ignite it and it'll flash back. You can do the same thing on the overhead; by heating the propane it'll go up and you can flash it across ceilings. A fireball is simply a puff of propane with a short cutoff on it. It's a calculated risk. You try to set up the physical effect so the chances are less of the actor getting hurt than they were riding in their limousine getting there. If you want to end your career real quick, injure an actor. Second, you don't want to injure a

---

138   Interview, "Hell Under Water, Fire in the Sky," op cit
139   Allen in studio publicity interview, op cit

stuntman, but you could probably survive injuring a stuntman. But injuring an actor, you're through."[140]

The pyrotechnicians used two distinct types of fuel: acetylene emitters for yellow, smoky flames, and butane emitters for blue, smokeless flames. These were augmented by air feeds and spark starters. For some scenes, cameras were fitted with remote controls to allow the crew to stand safely distant.

Irwin Allen's most frequent command when directing the action scenes was "More fire! More fire!" To keep both the flames and Allen under control, Thane Morris noted, "The fire guys work with you. They're often the hammer on the set where the director goes a little goofy and says, "I want to do such-and-such" and you don't think it's safe, the director or the producer can fire the effects guy but he can't fire the fireman."

Because fire scenes could go on for only a short time, the man who filmed them, Joe Biroc, commanded between three and eight cameras for each shot, hiding them from each other and figuring that, among them, they would generate enough footage at varying speeds for editors Carl and Harold Kress to piece together into an exciting sequence.[141]

The most realistic looking stunts were those involving people on fire; this was because stunt performers really were set on fire. To do this, the performer donned insulated, fire-retardant clothing and wore an oxygen mask hidden behind a face mask molded to resemble the actor being doubled. Because the air supply and fire protection were severely short-lived, spotters were stationed to extinguish the performer as soon as the director called "cut."

Irwin Allen was maniacal about safety on his films, but he also wanted audiences to think that his actors were truly in peril. "The principles were definitely near the fire," said Robert Vaughn, who played the stylishly corrupt Senator Gary Parker, "but, as you know, in filming, depth perception is very cagey

---

140   Interviewed in *Hell Under Water, Fire in the Sky*, op cit.

141   David Hammond, "'Action Unit' Lives Up to Its Name While Shooting 'The Towering Inferno,'" *American Cinematographer* magazine, February 1975.

where you're using a camera. You can make something look like it's much closer than it is, so you can give the illusion of proximity much worse or better than it actually is in terms of the actor being close to the fire. I don't think there was anybody that close or they would have stopped the camera and re-shot it or re-staged it so they wouldn't take a chance because they had too many valuable money-makers in star roles in that picture. I couldn't imagine anything being more spectacular than that particular film in terms of scaring an audience, and that's what they intended to do, and they did. It scared me, anyway."[142]

Much to the concern of Allen, the studios, and the insurance company, Steve McQueen insisted on doing many of his own stunts, including the helicopter descent to the scenic elevator and donning an insulated suit to walk through fire. Granted, the scenic elevator stunt was on a mock-up only a few feet off the ground, but it was still a possible fall. As for walking through fire in a stairwell when McQueen uses a door to shield himself from flames, it should be remembered that Paul Newman was walking right behind him without any protection. But McQueen knew something that Allen also knew: audiences pay to see a star's face. For this reason, whenever technical advisors told Allen that a real fire would generate more smoke, he reminded them that his cast needed to be seen. Said Allen, "Every actor that was aboard was alerted to the fact that we would be working very close to fire. There was a fifty million dollar insurance policy taken out, a special insurance policy, in the case of any difficulty involving the actors. They were all warned. Happily, no one was hurt."[143]

Allen and Guillermin had different directing styles, to say the least. Witnesses—perhaps exaggerating, perhaps not—reported that Allen's most frequent instruction on his scenes was "More fire! More fire! Bigger!" Guillermin, on the other hand, knew how to play each actor like a harp.

---

142   Interviewed in *Hell Under Water, Fire in the Sky,* op cit.
143   Irwin Allen studio publicity interview, 1977.

"Irwin did direct me in a second unit scene," recalled Susan Blakely, most of whose scenes were directed by Guillermin. "He was fun to work with. Before we shot the breeches buoy scene [where she is evacuated in an aerial bucket hanging 138 stories high]—I was working myself up to be scared as actors often do. I remember him saying to me, "'Relax, it's okay.' I had to say, 'Irwin, this is just me getting myself into it. I'll be okay.'"[144]

"His relationship with Paul Newman was really, really interesting to watch on the set," recalled Richard Chamberlain. "They'd get into knock down, drag out argument before every one of Paul's scenes. They'd start arguing about it: 'it's got to be this way,' 'no, it's got to be. . .,' 'John!,' 'Paul!' and then suddenly [John would] say, 'action' and Paul would be in the scene and do the scene and be terrific. And I suddenly twigged to the fact that this was how Paul liked to warm up. I don't know if he did this on other films, but on this film he would pick a fight with the director and the director totally saw what was happening, and then he'd slide right into it without pause, right into it, into shooting the scene. Fascinating."[145]

Susan Blakely, making only her fourth film, noted of Allen, "That's kind of what I remember: him yelling, 'More fire, more fire!' He was just such a character. What's interesting is that John Guillermin was different, very English and reserved. He totally trusted the actors. My impression was that he was really stressed and busy even though he was quiet. He had a lot on his plate. It was one of the most expensive movies ever made at the time."[146]

The film's climax, in which water tanks on the roof are exploded to drown the fire, was nearly as dangerous to shoot as it was in the story. "It did involve all of the actors," Allen said, "because, being the climax of the [film], they all had to be present. Who was gonna live? Who was gonna die? Who would be seriously hurt (for story purposes, not in reality). I would say that was the most difficult scene. We did have nine cameras. I take great pride

---

144 Author interview July 13, 2022

145 2003 DVD special feature on John Guillermin.

146 Author interview July 13, 2022.

in that particular scene because it was a scene that I directed. It took us nine days to photograph what was on the screen for just about nine minutes. We're kind of proud of it. We're proud that everybody lived through it, including me."[147]

"The greatest number of cameras were used on the giant promenade set," wrote David Hammond in *American Cinematographer*,[148] "which covered an entire sound stage." Measuring 11,000 square feet, it was constructed with removable ceiling panels for lighting access, as were many of the main fire sets. A 360-foot cyclorama of the San Francisco skyline surrounded this massive set.[149] Director of Photography Joseph Biroc "isolate[d] at least one camera on each of the main characters and one or two others on the elements that they would have to contend with during that sequence—fire, water, and explosions, sometimes all three."

Hammond notes eight cameras in use and three weeks to get it all on film, made complicated because the ceilings had to be seen and that's where they usually hide the lights. "The water actually used during the sequence was kept overhead in 12,000-gallon capacity tanks. The flow was directed along chutes, which guided it to the entry points on the ceiling. Special effects expert A.D. Flowers was able to pinpoint exactly where the main force would hit . . .but not where it would splash or flow. The [camera] operators worked in bathing suits and rain gear." At one point Allen himself got soaked by standing too close to the action.

With a large star cast it's astonishing that there were few reports of clashing egos (or perhaps Allen's was so great as to smother anybody else's). According to Ernie Orsatti (and backed up by production reports included in the *Backstory*[150] documentary episode on the making of the film), Faye Dunaway developed a habit of showing up late to shoot her few scenes, and some-

---

147   ibid

148   David Hammond, "Filming the Action Sequences for *The Towering Inferno*," *American Cinematographer*, February 1975.

149   Bob Fisher, "*The Towering Inferno* and How It Was Filmed," *American Cinematographer*, February 1975.

150   2003 DVD special features

times didn't appear at all. Finally she was given a stern talking-to by William Holden for her unprofessional behavior and was on time thereafter.

On two instances, McQueen showed the personal mettle for which his screen characters were always known. When an actual fire broke out on one of the sets, the actor, still in his fire chief's uniform, pitched in to help the real firefighters. Only when it was out did the pros realize who it was who'd helped them. On another occasion one of the fire hoses broke loose and started flailing around the set, threatening to douse everything within range, including the cameras. Crew member Gary King tried to control it, but this was no garden hose (as seen in newsreels of police aiming them at civilians) and he soon found himself outmatched. Here McQueen rushed in and helped King get control of the errant hose. The actor even lent King some of his dry clothes.[151]

---

151 "Starts at 60," July 12, 2016. https://startsat60.com/media/opinion/nostalgia/the-behind-the-scenes-drama-of-1974s-the-towering-inferno. Of note is that, unlike some stars, McQueen didn't notify the press when he performed his heroics; it leaked out after a time.

Chapter 10 Sidebar: Synopsis of *The Towering Inferno*

A helicopter carrying Doug Roberts[152] (Paul Newman), a high-end industrial architect, cruises along the San Francisco skyline and lands atop the 138-story, 1,688-foot skyscraper he has designed for his old friend, real estate magnate James Duncan (William Holden). The Glass Tower, as the building is called, is the world's tallest structure and it dominates the San Francisco skyline. Tonight is the tower's VIP-heavy dedication in the Promenade Room on the 135th floor. Roberts has been elsewhere working on an environmental project rather than supervising the final phase of construction and wants to return to the land. Duncan tries to entice him to stay with promise of a huge contract for urban renewal.

Roberts is surprised in his 79th floor office by Susan Thompson (Faye Dunaway), a journalist whose impending promotion—and desire to have a career—means that their relationship may be ending because she doesn't want to move with him to Montana. He is also assailed by building supervisors who tell him that the tower's exhaust dampers won't stay open and other test-run glitches.

Harlee Claiborne (Fred Astaire) arrives and stiffs his cab driver for a tip.

Artist/heiress Lisolette Mueller (Jennifer Jones) finishes a messy art class with two kids whose deaf mother takes them away.

As engineers test the building's electrical system, an exploding fuse on the 81st floor sparks an unseen fire in a supply closet. Security officer Harry Jernigan (O.J. Simpson)

152　In all versions of the script until the last one, Newman's character is named Craig Wilson, an amalgam from the two source books. It was likely changed for legal reasons, i.e. there was a real architect named Craig Wilson and the company wanted to avoid a lawsuit. In any event, "Doug Roberts" is the name of the beloved main character in the play and film *Mister Roberts* by Joshua Logan and Thomas Heggen.

notices an anomaly on the complex alert board but the heat sensor does not automatically call the fire department.

Investigating the reason for the short circuit, Roberts discovers that substandard materials have been used in construction. He confronts Duncan with questions about what other corners may have been cut. As they stew, the company's PR man Dan Bigelow (Robert Wagner) arrives and learns that they could have had a fire. Engineer Callahan (John Crawford) echoes Roberts' concerns and adds that the safety equipment hasn't been fully installed yet. Duncan hastily puts out a call to his son-in-law, Roger Simmons (Richard Chamberlain), the building contractor. When he can't be located, Roberts goes to the mansion[153] of Simmons and Duncan's daughter, Patty (Susan Blakely) and challenges Simmons. Simmons says that the building is up to Code, and Roberts counters that his specs required materials above Code. Not only that, Patti's and Roger's marriage is in trouble.

People arrive for the building dedication. Harlee, a broke but stylish con man, has wangled an invitation and calls for Lisolette (who has a cat named Elke) to take her to the event.

Crowds assemble at the base of the building for celebrity arrivals: Senator Gary Parker (Robert Vaughn),the Simmonses, and Mayor and Mrs. Robert Ramsay (Jack Collins and Sheila Mathews) who cut the ribbon. On Bigelow's signal, Callahan turns on all the structure's lights, overloading the electrical system. At the same time, fire has consumed unnoticed the supply room on the 81st floor. Bigelow asks his secretary, Lorrie (Susan Flannery) to stay and take a letter. Soon we see that she is taking more than dictation; the two are lovers.

The party is in progress. A singer (Maureen McGovern) sings "We May Never Love Like This Again." Duncan bribes

---

153 Located at 2898 Vallejo Street in tony Pacific Heights district. Its fellow residents include writer-killer Catherine Tramell's (Sharon Stone's) home in *Basic Instinct* (1992; 2930 Vallejo) and crooked politician Chalmers's (Robert's Vaughn's) in *Bullitt* (1968; 2700 Vallejo). There goes the neighborhood.

Parker with a case of rare wine; Simmons hits on Susan; Harlee charms Lisolette.

Roberts demands that all the extra lights be shut down. At Security they finally notice the fire on 81 and call the San Francisco Fire Department.

On floor 81 a guard sees smoke coming from the utility room. He starts to open the door. Engineer Giddings (Normann Burton) pushes him aside as it opens but is himself engulfed in flame, which Parker rushes to smother with nearby drapes. Roberts is shocked at seeing Callahan's injuries but Jernigan breaks his stupor and tells him to call an ambulance.

Roberts informs Duncan of the fire. Duncan insists he's overreacting and won't clear the top floor, thinking the building to be fireproof.

Two firefighters (Ernie Orsatti and Felton Perry), en route to the fire, are stunned that their destination is the Glass Tower. When the fleet arrives, Fire Chief Mike O'Hallorhan (Steve McQueen) instantly takes charge. Firefighter Kappy (Don Gordon) brings Roberts to O'Hallorhan who briefs him. They set up command on the 79th floor. O'Hallorhan makes the point that firefighters can't fight a fire above the seventh floor and gives a quick fire hazard education to Jernigan, Roberts, and the audience. Roberts suggests that O'Hallorhan make Duncan evacuate the party. When Duncan resists, O'Hallorhan demands it. Duncan then gets Simmons who confesses to cutting corners but blames it on Duncan's orders to slash costs. Duncan informs the guests they must move to the Continental room many floors below.

Meanwhile, the firefighters are unable to control the fire on 81. There is an explosion, the ceiling blows, the flames erupt from the center of the building. The fire hits the elevators. Several guests take them, not realizing that the cabs will home to the fire floor where it opens and they are incinerated.

Lisolette manages to get to the floor where the two children and their mother live, The deaf mother cannot hear her knocking on the door.

A man emerges on flames from the elevator and Harlee smothers them with the jacket of his rented tux. Guests faint; Duncan stews.

Bigelow and Lorrie get dressed and prepare to go their separate ways, she home and he to the party. When they find themselves trapped by fames, Bigelow lifts the phone to summon rescue, then realizes that he has turned them off for privacy. Trying to persuade Lorrie that he will fetch help, he puts a wet towel on his head and rushes to his flaming death. Lorrie knows she will be next. She breaks the window with a chair and becomes a human fireball, plunging to her death.

Jernigan goes to fetch the deaf woman and her kids. He, Lisolette, and Roberts rescue the mother and children from their smoky apartment as more engine companies arrive.

Duncan and Parker try to sneak down the stairwells. One is smoky, the other is sealed shut by a load of cement dumped there by workmen.

When O'Hallorhan calls for men to climb stairwells, every firefighter steps forward. They must ascend the building by stairs carrying thirty to fifty pounds of gear including breathing equipment.

Jernigan finds Elke (Lisolette's cat).

At any moment a situation can change. As Roberts leads Lisolette and the children down the stairwell, a gas main explodes, wrecking the stairwell and separating them. They head up to the Promenade Room only to find the door shut with dried cement. Roberts ventures to the roof through dangerous ductwork, making it to the Promenade Room while the others wait.

The master generator blows. The external scenic elevator that people were using to descend is now stuck on the top floor and can be used only once to descend by gravity. Who will get to enter it? All systems have now failed.

A firefighter falls to his death, afire, down the elevator shaft. Another firefighter (Scott Newman) is afraid to rappel down the elevator shaft. O'Hallorhan tells him to go first so he doesn't take anyone else with him. He will make it.

Navy helicopters arrive but it's too windy to land on the roof. Firefighters blow open the blocked exit but inform Duncan and the others that the stairway is gone. Lisolette and the kids enter and Carlos (Gregory Sierra) the friendly bartender, gives them sodas.

O'Hallorhan wants to hook up a breeches buoy (transfer bucket) by cable from the nearby Peerless building.

Susan and Roberts have a moment. Patty and Simmons do not. Harlee confesses his poverty to Lisolette; she doesn't care.

Duncan insists to Roberts that he kept within the building code. Roberts tells him that his plans exceeded the code for safety reasons and he lays it on Simmons.

More explosions, more floors gone. A fifth fire company is summoned.

The mayor and his wife have a moment. They are preparing to die.

Susan numbers paper stubs for a lottery for the escape order.

When the first chopper tries to land on the roof, two guests rush it and it crashes and explodes. The dangerous breeches buoy is now the only way to safety.

Roberts fills the scenic elevator with twelve people including Lisolette (who saved the children), a fireman (Ernie Orsatti), and ten others who drew lots, including Susan and the mayor's wife.

As the beeches buoy is connected, an explosion rocks the scenic elevator off its track. Lisolette falls to her death. The others hang there suspended. O'Hallorhan takes a helicopter from the roof of the shorter Peerless building and picks up the dangling elevator, almost losing the fireman in the process.

A Deputy chief (Dabney Colman) suggests that O'Hallorhan volunteer to blow up the water tanks atop the

Glass Tower, releasing a million gallons of water to drown the fire. The bad news is that he will have no way to get down if it fails.[154] O'Hallorhan informs Roberts that the fire is out of control and they have fifteen minutes before it reaches them. He tells him the water tank plan.

With all the women now safely evacuated in the breeches buoy, Simmons leads a rush to it and he, Senator Parker, and others plunge to the street.

O'Hallorhan and Roberts plant charges under the huge water storage tanks on the floor above the Promenade Room. All who remain in the room (i.e. the stars) lash themselves to a pillar or other secure place. The tanks explode just as the fire reaches them. Some people untie themselves and try to flee and are blown through windows by the force of the water. The flood quells the fire. Survivors include O'Hallorhan, Roberts, Harlee, Duncan, Susan, Patty, and Mayor Ramsay. The body count is less than two hundred. Jernigan finds Harlee and give him Lisolette's cat. O'Hallorhan sees the covered bodies of dead firefighters.

On the street, as the fire units pack to leave, O'Hallorhan admonishes Roberts that architects should ask firemen how to build safe buildings. Roberts, sitting beside an admiring Susan, agrees.

Chapter 10 Sidebar: Deleted Scenes

Most movies shoot more footage than they need but it isn't always clear which scenes can be removed until the whole picture can be viewed in rough cut. With The Tower-

---

154 Of this moment, observed *Inferno* fan Teller (of Penn & Teller), "when McQueen's told that someone needs to get on top of the building and blow up the water tanks, and he says, 'And how does that guy get out of there?' Then there's a silence from the guy proposing the idea, and McQueen responds, 'Shit.' In that one Steve McQueen 'shit,' you get the essence of his character, who's the most American sort of heroic character you could possibly imagine." (Interviewed by Noel Murray for *Dissolve*, June 12, 2014.)

ing Inferno *it was clear that a running time of over three-hours was going to be untenable (as it is, it's two hours and forty-four minutes with no intermission), so the editors went to work making it shorter and more efficient. As they are for any film, cuts were made with three considerations:*

1. *Does the scene advance the story or does it repeat something covered elsewhere?*
2. *Does the scene concisely convey its information or are there extra moments?*
3. *Does the scene play effectively?*

In addition, The Towering Inferno had to consider whether losing or keeping a scene would violate the contracts of its stars who required equal screen time or an equal number of lines. (William Holden and Faye Dunaway lost the most in that regard.)

Approximately twenty minutes of these deleted scenes were restored for the film's initial television airing in two two-hour blocks on February 17 and 18, 1980 on NBC. In retrospect, these cuts would have enriched character but not significantly advanced the plot. Other trims were simple scene extensions or cutaways of firefighters fighting flames, engines racing through city streets, and people walking across rooms or waiting for elevators):

- Roberts and Susan in the bedroom that Susan Thompson has designed for them in Roberts's office. Roberts wants Susan to join him in his Montana retreat while she wants to keep her journalism career.[155]
- Scenes 39-48 and 175-181 the Second Revised Final shooting script may have been shot but never made it into the final cut. They are of Chief O'Hallorhan testifying before a municipal panel about fire codes and how they are inadequate for high-rises. "I will tell

---

155 Susan is the only main character with no assigned last name in the film (in the script it's "Thompson"). Moreover, despite being a journalist, she is completely indifferent to covering what must be the biggest breaking news story of her career.

you one thing," he says to "Presiding Officer," "in this whole city–and we've got the best fire code in the country–there aren't five buildings I'd let my wife and kids go into–unless they stayed on the first floor." Soon thereafter we meet O'Hallorhan's wife Dorothy, his son Michael, and their toddler. This scene would have occurred fifteen minutes into the picture. The second cut O'Hallorhan scene is set on the family's houseboat where Mike and Michael are about to set out in their dinghy to catch fish at night. A phone call summons him to the tower fire. Neither cut scene is necessary for the plot but they do establish and enrich character. Losing them meant that McQueen wouldn't make his entrance until forty-six minutes into the film where-as Newman had been there practically from the first shot. What this did to the balance of lines between them is best left to their agents to debate.

- Mr. Richard (Malcolm Atterbury), the jeweler, delivers the golden ribbon-cutting scissors to Dan Bigelow. Bigelow is in a staff meeting arranging seating for the dinner. He procures a case of rare wine for Senator Parker, thanks his secretary (Susan Flannery), accepts the scissors, and realizes they forgot to order the big broad ribbon that it will slice.
- After Roberts warns Duncan about the fire, Duncan wonders aloud to Bigelow that perhaps they should have put off the party a month.
- Giddings tells Jernigan that their whole security program is "loused up" without the electrical system working properly.
- Harlee calls for Lisolette and starts laying it on. Harlee's entrance was to have occurred well after the a start of the fire, but was moved up in editing to get Fred Astaire and Jennifer Jones into the story sooner.

- Duncan wants Susan to help him keep Roberts working for him designing buildings despite Roberts's desire to head to the wilderness. Susan declines.
- Mayor Ramsay's speech is extended.
- Duncan invites the mayor and senator Parker to ride the observation elevator and admits that only one of the three is functioning. As they ascend, senator Parker (Robert Vaughn) boasts that the building was completed without federal help.
- Maureen McGovern sings more of her song ("We May Never Love Like this Again") at the party.
- At the party, Susan counsels Patty about men that get away, then Roger Simmons joins them. Patty later tells Susan that Roberts visited her and Roger at their home that afternoon to complain about the electrical contracting.
- The building's reception area is on fire starting with a shot that begins on a sign reading "We Build for Life" as a forth alarm is sounded.
- Patty thanks her father for her happy childhood.
- Lisolette, waiting for Roberts to rescue them from the stairwell, distracts the children Angela (Carlena Gower) and Philip (Mike Lookinland) with finger shadows.
- One controversial scene that vanished after a sneak preview involves the young firefighter who was afraid to rappel down the elevator shaft (scene 359-360) as covered in the synopsis. When Allen saw the footage, he was so impressed with young Scott Newman that he told him, "You were so good that we're going to kill you." He then had Silliphant write a scene in which the young firefighter accidentally grabs a live electric cable and is electrocuted. He dies in O'Hallorhan's arms. The scene stayed in through one sneak preview in Hartford, Connecticut but was cut because,

on reconsideration, Allen was concerned that it suggested that firefighters could make such a mistake.[156]

There were other deletions and changes during production, some of them creative and others reflecting simply the way business is done. A comparison of the shooting script with the finished film shows that almost every line of dialogue is changed in one way or another: words are excised, added, and rearranged. Some of these are so the dialogue would rest more comfortably in the actors' mouths. Some were cut during editing to speed the scene along; that is, once an editorial pace is established, the film very often doesn't need as many words. Just get on with it.

And then there's a third reason. Actors (and not just McQueen and Newman) count their lines. It's a well-known practice for writers to pad an actor's part in the script knowing full well that the extra lines will be cut in post-production. This is why many actors feel that making movies is not as satisfying as theatre acting because once their job is done their work lives or dies at the hands of editors, directors, and sound mixers. The rule of thumb is that one page of script equals one minute of screen time, but *The Towering Inferno*'s shooting script, at 156 pages, describes so many action scenes that, had all of it been filmed and assembled, it would have run over four hours. The final film runs two hours and forty-four minutes. Something had to go, and what better material to lose than that which was planned never to be in the movie anyway?

Chapter 10: Sidebar: The Other Director

As the story goes, an interviewer asked producer Samuel Goldwyn, "When William Wyler made *Wuthering Heights—*" when Goldwyn forcefully cut him off and said, "*I* made

---

156 Disclosed to the author by Scott Newman whom the author represented on press appearances.

Wuthering Heights. Wyler only directed it." The same might be said for John Guillermin who, quoting the publicity, "directed the dramatic scenes" for *The Towering Inferno* but is barely mentioned in any of the interviews or press reports for his film. Instead, Irwin Allen, who produced and directed the action sequences, receives the bulk of the coverage. It implies that Guillermin was some kind of hack, which he wasn't, or was content to stay in the background, which wasn't the case, either. It seems simply that Guillermin was a pragmatist, having gone in with his eyes wide open that, on an Irwin Allen production, the star is Irwin Allen.

Besides, he had nothing to prove. Not only was his ego secure, so were his diplomatic skills; how otherwise could he juggle star egos while keeping up with a crushing shooting schedule, all of which stand as silent tribute to his expertise. When asked about the demarcation in duties, Guillermin expressed a simple, pragmatic answer: "This is Irwin's movie." At the same time, he asserted silent control over his scenes by cutting in the camera, that is, ending shots at the precise point where he wanted the splices to come, thus providing the editors with only just enough footage to construct his scenes his way. This drove Allen crazy.[157]

Guillermin, 44 when he directed *Inferno*, came to blockbusters after surviving one in real life. That was World War Two, when he joined in the RAF in his native England at age 19, dropping out of Cambridge University. He served three years, then went to France (though born in England, his parents were French) and got a job making documentaries. Returning to England, he continued making films, mostly low-budget "quota quickies" that entertained British audiences when Hollywood films weren't on the bill. The few that were picked up for distribution in America were handled by several companies—MGM, Columbia, Allied Artists—until

---

157 Jeff Bond, *The Fantasy Worlds of Irwin Allen*, CA: Creature Features, 2019.

his taut 1964 drama *Guns at Batasi* was seen by Twentieth Century-Fox studio head Darryl F. Zanuck. Zanuck was impressed enough with the young Brit to hire him to direct Fox's World War I picture, *The Blue Max* (1966). Its exciting aerial sequences and tense ground drama assured Guillermin of a Hollywood career and began a long friendship with actor George Peppard. The two men wound up making two more pictures together, the detective yarn *P.J.* and the espionage adventure *House of Cards* (both 1968).

Tall, angular, fit, and pipe-smoking, Guillermin looked for all the world like the husband in Disney's *One Hundred and One Dalmatians*. Those who worked with him said he was tough but fair, excitable but pragmatic, and patient when patience was called for. He had a hair-trigger temper but it was quickly calmed, and his crews accepted this as an expression of his creative energy. A commander with his crews but distant with his actors, he got the job done.

"I thought he was quite amazing," said Susan Blakely, "because. . .of the organization of it. It was like being a general in an army."[158]

"John was a very quiet man," praised Fred Koenekamp, his *Inferno* cinematographer. "If he showed any temper it was in a nice, quiet way. He would want something done now and so forth, where Irwin was just the opposite. When Irwin walked on the set, everybody knew he was there."[159]

"He was good as a director," adds Susan Flannery, speaking of Allen, "but Guillermin, in all honesty, had a different instinct as a director."[160]

He was comfortable in any genre he was handed: war (*Bridge at Remagen*, 1969), comic book heroics (*Tarzan Goes to India*, 1962), elegant mystery (*Death on the Nile*, 1978), and high adventure (*El Condor*, 1970). Although he never made an outright comedy, *Sheena, Queen of the*

---

158   2003 DVD special feature on John Guillermin.
159   2003 DVD special feature on John Guillermin.
160   ibid

Jungle (1984) comes close. He also had the guts to remake the cinema classic *King Kong* (1933) not just once (1975) but with a sequel (*King Kong Lives*, 1986). Although his personal favorite was the quiet British drama *Rapture* (1965),[161] he was best known for action films, a type of high-pressure production that requires flawless organization and keen focus on logistics, often to the exclusion of the needs of the people in front of the camera. This is why he was at easy with stars, among them Charlton Heston, Orson Welles, Peter Sellers, Peter Ustinov, and other established personalities who had their own ways of working.

Perhaps it was the airborne group jeopardy film *Skyjacked* (1972) that brought him to Irwin Allen's attention. Although the delineation between each man's domain was clear—Guillermin handled the actors except where fire or stunts were involved, in which case the megaphone was passed to Allen—there is no knowing what arrangements they and their egos may have made in private. What is important is that the footage that Guillermin shot with his director of photography Fred Koenekamp and that Allen shot with his director of photography L.B. Abbott meshed seamlessly so that the resulting film has a consistency of style, color, and integrity.

Guillermin was no pushover. As his widow, Mary (they were married from 1998 until his death in 2015), told interviewer Stephen Vagg on the occasion of the publication of her book[162] about her late husband, "He felt like a frustrated artist. He felt he had many more films like *Rapture* in him but because of his temperament and the way he lived his life (he took the work that came to support his family) he knew he had unused talent. He was modest." Guillermin was subject to depression, in part because of the breakup of his first marriage (to Maureen Connell) but also from the death of his son, Michael, who had been working on his father's *Shee-*

---

161   A young woman has an unusual relationship with an escaped convict.
162   Mary Guillermin et al., *John Guillermin: The Man, The Myth, The Movies* (Brentwood, California: Precocity Press, 2020).

na film crew in Africa before leaving for America, where he died in a car accident. The two had become estranged and never got to make rapprochement.

Said his widow, who pulled him from his depression, "I thought there was a lot of art in his films. At some point, I started looking to see what there was written about him. Only a few paragraphs here and there, and they were entirely about his temper. The whole entry on Wikipedia was about his bad temper. After his death it was fuller, but I knew he wouldn't want to be known just for *The Towering Inferno*."[163] She wrote her book, inviting others to contribute, to correct that.

It is ironic, therefore, that, despite all his achievements, IMDb identifies him as the director of *The Towering Inferno*, perhaps his least spiritually representative film.

John Guillermin died of a heart attack at home in Topanga Canyon, California, on September 27, 2015 at age 89. His wife Mary and daughter Michelle, by Maureen Connell, survived him.

Chapter 10 Sidebar: Factoids

The paintings in Jennifer Jones's apartment set are authentic. Several valuable pieces, including three Picassos, were loaned to the production by collector Norton Simon to add elegance to Lisolette's plush living quarters. The loan was easy to arrange since Jones was married to him. It was also rumored that Simon—a large Fox stockholder—leaned on the studio to hire his wife once Olivia de Havilland turned down the role.

Before shooting the culminating flooding scene in the Promenade Room set, Steve McQueen joked, "If anything

---

163 Stephen Vagg, Film Ink, January 3, 2021. https://www.filmink.com.au/john-guillermin-the-man-the-myth-the-movies/

happens to me, Ali gets my pickup truck." McQueen was married to actress Ali MacGraw at the time. This moment was captured in a behind-the-scenes featurette and McQueen was concerned that the line might make him look frivolous. No, insisted those he asked about it, it makes you look human.

In order to capture the actors' surprised expressions as the water tanks explode during the film's big finish, Irwin Allen counted down from ten to one and, somewhere along the way, fired a pistol to shock them.

Steve McQueen didn't like the shape of his fire fighter's helmet; the brim was too big and would hide his face, so he had one made with a narrow lip. This also made it easier to light him. He's the only fire fighter in the entire film with such an abbreviated brim.

Not wanting to fake it with prop equipment, McQueen insisted on wearing the immensely heavy gear that firefighters routinely carry with them into fires. He later said it was the one piece of wardrobe he didn't want to take home with him after the film wrapped. (Yes, stars frequently get to keep their wardrobe.)

McQueen left orders with unit publicist Don Morgan that he didn't want to be bothered by interviewers visiting the set. So did Faye Dunaway. As for Paul Newman, he reportedly said he'd meet with visiting press but to let him know first so he wouldn't be ambushed.

When Fred Astaire and Jennifer Jones dance in the ballroom scene, Astaire—easily the screen's greatest dancer—purposely looked clumsy so as not to intimidate Jones, who could not dance nearly as well. Before Astaire was hired, there was talk of casting David Niven or Peter Ustinov.

Technically, Steve McQueen and Faye Dunaway co-star in *The Towering Inferno* just as they had in 1968's *The Thomas Crown Affair*. Yet in the one scene they have together, she is not present. Her character is in the damaged scenic elevator that McQueen hangs from a helicopter to rescue, but it's probably a female stunt performer taking her place and the two of them never even share a shot.

Smoke that was not the result of a fire—that is, smoke used in closeups and isolated shots of actors—was actually made from burning wood chips, untreated burlap, cotton fuel pellets, and untreated bailing twine. This is what bee keepers use to calm their hives. There are no reports as to whether this same blend calmed the actors. The smoke was also kept to unrealistically low levels so that audiences could still see the actors' faces.

At least four marriages took place during or shortly after filming: Faye Dunaway and musician Peter Wolf, Ernie Orsatti and model Lynda Farrell, writer Stirling Silliphant and actress Tiana Alexandra, and Irwin Allen and Sheila Mathews.

Shots placing foreground action shot in the studio against background action involving miniatures was done in the lab using then-standard "blue screen" compositing. The problem with blue screen is that if anyone wears blue clothes or has blue eyes (viz Newman and McQueen), those features can become transparent and allow the background to show through. In 1959 Peter Vlahos invented green screen, bright green being less prevalent in eyes and clothes, which was first used in the film *Ben-Hur*. Vlahos later received an Oscar® for his compositing work in *Mary Poppins* (1964).[164]

---

164 Uncredited, American Movie Company website: https://www.american-movieco.com/greenscreenstudio/petro-vlahos-inventor-of-green-screen-blue-screen-technology-dies/

At the end of the film, Chief O'Hallorhan casts a mournful gaze at the covered remains of nine fire fighters who died fighting the fire.

For exterior scenes during the fire sequences, Allen hired, in addition to twenty-five professional stunt performers under stunt coordinator Paul Stader, up to seventy-five off-duty firefighters from surrounding stations. Not only were the real firefighters available as technical advisors, they were there in case anything actually got out of control.

It is never explained how the drenched survivors of the fire got down to the ground from the Promenade Room.

Kudos should be given to Directors of Photography Fred J. Koenekamp and Joseph Biroc for their skill in filming a movie about an incredibly tall object that stands up and down despite the widescreen Panavision process that goes side to side.

The song sung by Maureen McGovern in the dedication party, "We May Never Love Like This Again," was written by Al Kasha and Joel Hirshhorn who also wrote the song "There's Got to Be a Morning After" for *The Poseidon Adventure* two years earlier. Both songs won Academy Awards®. "We May Never Love Like This Again" may have been helped toward its Oscar® victory because Fox mailed free copies of *The Towering Inferno* soundtrack album, with music composed by John Williams, to all of the then-5,000 Academy members.

It isn't that Paul Newman wasn't as competitive as Steve McQueen, he just kept it inside or called his agent. The two had been friendly rivals since they were both up for the part of Rocky Graziano in the 1956 Robert Wise film *Somebody*

Up There Likes Me. When James Dean, who was originally to have played Rocky, was killed in a car crash in 1955, Newman won the role and McQueen never forgot it.

Chapter 10 Sidebar: Susie Blakely

Susan "Susie" Blakely was a top fashion model in New York and had begun making acting appearances (Savages, 1972; The Way We Were, 1973; and The Lords of Flatbush, 1974) when she was cast in a key role as an undercover cop in Report to the Commissioner (released in 1975). Report was still shooting in 1974 when Allen was sent rushes of her scenes by producer Mike Frankovich. Allen was so impressed that he cast her as Patty Simmons, the wife of the corrupt contractor Roger Simmons (Richard Chamberlain) and daughter of building developer Jim Duncan (William Holden).

Her youth at the time of filming The Towering Inferno *gave her some wonderful memories:*

"If I had known there would be all these interviews I would have paid more attention! It's very difficult for me to watch anything that I'm in, and I was nervous being on that set with so many big stars because I was just starting off.

"Paul Newman was very friendly. Bill Holden, too. We went to lunch together sometimes. We would often go to the commissary but we also went to the Apple Pan[165] a lot—it was one of Bill Holden's favorite spots. Paul Newman and Joanne Woodward were so very gracious. They invited us out to their place in Malibu. They both really went out of their way. I really loved Joanne Woodward. She helped me get over my schoolgirl crush on Paul Newman. I was so glad she came to the set with him at the beginning to say 'hello.' She was so cool and down to earth. I got right over my crush—and, by the way, she was one of my favorite actresses growing up. She was actually one of the reasons I became and actress.

---

165   The Apple Pan is a classic Los Angeles diner: https://theapplepan.com/

When I was a kid growing up in Germany ["army brat"] I remember when I was nine I went to a matinee and got to see *The Three Faces of Eve*. Before that I always wanted to be a comedian because of Lucille Ball, and then when I saw Joanne do that part, even at a young age, I was profoundly affected. I thought it was an incredible role. Later, when I met her, she just couldn't have been nicer, so darling. She tried to teach me to knit because she used to knit on the set to help pass the time, but I didn't have the patience. Years later, we did a talk show together, *The Dinah Shore Show*, and it was so wonderful to see her again.

"While I was aware of Fred Astaire's immense reputation I had not seen a single one of his films. I stayed around after I'd finished shooting just to watch his scenes. I remember, after a scene one day, sitting on the stairs with him in between takes. He was genuinely humble. He'd ask me about a scene he'd just finished and ask, 'Do you think that was good?' It was odd that he was asking me! Little did I realize what an extraordinary moment that was in my life. One weekend there was a retrospective of his films at a theater nearby. I went to it and came out in shock. He was a genius. When I got back to the set, I could hardly speak to him.

"Paul Newman really went out of his way to be nice to people but I do remember one time when we were in San Francisco at a Moroccan restaurant where he'd invited me, Richard Chamberlain, and Robert Vaughn to join him. A woman came over to the table totally drunk. She had these long white gloves on and she said, 'Paul! Paul!' as she hung her arms on him. 'I bet my friends that you would invite me to sit down,' she said. He tried to be nice, but finally removed her arm from his shoulder and said, 'Lady, you need to go back to your table and sit down.'

"Bill Holden, who I adored, was warm and friendly except when he was eating in a public place. Of course, this was my first time seeing this kind of reaction to such world-famous people. Even in the days when I was a top model there weren't paparazzi or people bothering you. I had some fame because I was known from some commercials where they would say, 'Cover Girl Susie Blakely,' but it wasn't anything like what these two superstars were subjected to. Bill really didn't like people bothering him while he was eating. He would go from being the nicest, funniest guy to, all of a sudden just freezing. I remember him being interrupted mid-sentence, holding his fork with food on it and waiting until the intruder stopped talking. Then he said to the person, "Are you finished? Good. Can I finish eating now?' It seemed strange to see that but then I thought, I have no idea what this must be like for him after decades of being a world-famous movie star. To have a life of people never leaving you alone. Also, we didn't have that long to eat. Normally, just 45 minutes.

"Steve McQueen was kind and tried to clue me in. He saw me right after I'd just come in from a costume fitting and make-up test. I had darkened my hair to look more frumpy because I thought I should look that way. My character was a rich, upper-class young woman who was married to a player. She was a person who hadn't been out in the world much and was very naïve, the kind of woman who would fall for a guy like her low-life husband. Irwin Allen didn't want me to wear my hair dark but I explained it to him and he kind of let me do it. So when Steve McQueen saw me walk in he said, 'don't let them make you look like that.' I said, 'What do you mean?' He said, 'I've seen you'–I had been friends with Ali MacGraw in New York[166]–and I explained to him why I was looking this way. Well, he was right and I was wrong and the only scene I look good in is the one where Paul comes to the house because my hair was down and I looked better. These people knew what they were doing. It was nice of him to be looking out for me that way."[167]

---

166 McQueen and MacGraw were married at the time.
167 Author interview with Susan Blakely.

Chapter 11: Crash and Burn

Irwin Allen loved daredevil stunts and deeply respected the men and women stunt performers who carried them off. He hired over ninety of them on *The Towering Inferno* under the guidance of stunt coordinator Paul Stader. Stader had worked with Allen for the first time on *The Poseidon Adventure* and would continue with him through *The Swarm* and *Beyond the Poseidon Adventure*.

Stader was a dynamo. A Missouri native who was on the University of Kansas football and swimming teams, he came to Hollywood after meeting Olympic swimming champions Johnny Weissmuller and Larry "Buster" Crabbe. Although he specialized in water stunts (such as diving off of cliffs for John Ford's *The Hurricane* in 1937), he became an all-around stunt performer, doubling for Kirk Alyn in the *Superman* serial and for hundreds of other actors between 1937 and his retirement in 1992. His first credit as stunt coordinator was on 1982's *Where Eagles Dare*. A stunt coordinator not only plans and rehearses the stunts but ensures the stunty performers' safety, checks rigging and air bags, and advises the director or second unit director how best to shoot them. Sometimes the stunt coordinator is also the second unit director (as opposed to the second assistant director, which is vastly different).

From *Where Eagles Dare*, Stader not only planned "gags" (which is what stunts are often called) or directed them himself. On *The Towering Inferno* he coordinated the stunts with producer Irwin Allen who was himself the second unit director, although contracts required that his billing be called "directing the action sequences."

Among stunts required for *Inferno* were fire, falls, rappelling, being blown through windows, dangling from ropes and helicopters, water, explosions, and anything else that would create screen thrills.

Of all the performers in the film, the one that resisted taking direction was fire. The ephemeral nature of flames makes them hard to photograph. The dazzling presence that is so hypnotic for people to watch in real life is lost in objective photographic technology. Although the pyrotechnics experts knew what they were doing, the fire itself didn't like being photographed.

In the days when motion pictures were made in black and white, capturing fire on film was merely a matter of controlling their transparency; if flames didn't show up, chemicals were simply added to increase their opacity. Color introduced different problems inasmuch as the color-sensitivity of the emulsion on color stock records certain colors differently that the eye perceives them.

For example, everyday makeup photographs differently than the way it looks on the street or indoors. It has to do with the kind of light that is used, the chemical nature of the film, or the electronic nature of the video. This is why stage, film, and video makeup need to adjust their transparency, reflectiveness, and tint in order to resolve accurately. The lighting (intensity, tint, color temperature) on stage and screen demand makeup of different density, transparency, and color saturation. Add to that the specifics of photochemical film emulsion or the balance of video camera sensors and what you see on the set is not always what you get on the screen.

This is particularly true with fire where, in addition to color, there are opacity issues. Shooting fire on film has challenged filmmakers since the beginning, not just photographically but safety-wise. "Back then, people were actually doing fire stunts," notes Teller (of Penn & Teller, masters of stage illusion), "so there's that thing that comes from the authenticity of actually doing those gags."[168] Having said that, Teller makes it clear that

---

168   Noel Murray, *The Dissolve*, June 12, 2014.

when he and Penn do their magic nobody is ever really in jeopardy even though it looks like they are; doing otherwise, both men say, would be morally irresponsible.

Times have changed from the early days when a crew member simply set fire to the set with a match and hoped the actor would run out before the film did. Today fire conditions are more controlled to the point of being able to be turned on and off like a gas stove. Modern movie fire is a combination of practical and computer-generated visual effects designed to make it look real to the viewer even if it doesn't look real "in person" on the set. There is still a gap, but it's closing.

In 1991 the movie *Backdraft* sought new areas for its dramatization of firefighters and arson, They devised a combination of alcohol, kerosene, diesel fuel, and propane for their fires and used a spray gun to ignite a stream of the brew to make a wall of fire. Because the alcohol flame burned cleanly, they also sprayed a mixture of smoke and cardboard flakes to simulate the ash that precipitates from a real fire. And just to keep a foot in the old school, they spread flammable rubber cement on the walls and furniture so the fire would form a track.[169]

The 2022 remake of Stephen King's *Firestarter* took the best of both practical and computer worlds to retell its story of a young girl who could command flames. As *Firestarter*'s director Keith Thomas told *Slashfilm*'s Anthony Orlando, "All the fire is real. Some of it gets a little enhanced with VFX (visual effects) to clean up things that we couldn't take care of, but the final act features a 40-foot flamethrower, and those people are really being hit by it. We had built that set specifically to do that stunt. They've got oxygen tanks under there, and that fire is hitting them. That room's a thousand degrees. Flames are coming up out of the roof. Everyone has to clear the set. It's a major undertaking to do that. But to me, it resonates in a way that CGI can't. It has to be a handshake between special effects and practical

---

169 *"Backdraft*'s Effects," Christopher Henrickson, *Entertainment Weekly*, June 14, 1991 (updated https://ew.com/article/1991/06/14/backdrafts-effects/).

and CG, and they have to work together. Otherwise, one is just sitting on top of the other, and it doesn't work."[170]

Teller is cautious about such assurances. "I guess you'd really have to test it out with me. You'd have to show me a digital fire gag and then show me a practical fire gag, and see whether I can tell the difference. But I fancy that the limitations of a real fire gag in some way affects the viewer. There's something about this feeling of, 'It doesn't look absolutely perfect.' If Paul Newman throws a wet towel over his head and then runs into a scene, you know it's a stuntman. There's something about making those individual pieces into one single action—which is the principle of montage, really—so even though you know *this* is a stunt guy, and you know *that* was Paul Newman, you put them together in your head, and your imagination is being enlisted in a very interesting and positive way. Again, I've seen some great modern digital special effects that I have absolutely no problem with. But there is something, I think, very visceral about the way *The Towering Inferno* was put together."[171]

"It's a point related to magic," he continues, "which, even at its most perfect, always has minuscule cracks and flaws. And there's where to look for the poignancy of magic — at its core, it's about the longing we all feel for a miracle."[172]

Ernest F. (Ernie) Orsatti was a stunt performer who made memorable contributions to both Irwin Allen's *The Poseidon Adventure* and *The Towering Inferno*. He's the fellow who took the backward fall into the skylight in *The Poseidon Adventure* (and who is incorrectly identified on the Special Edition DVD commentary as the elevator rappeler). In *Inferno*, Orsatti played "Mark," the young firefighter saved by Chief O'Hallorhan from falling to his death during the tense scenic elevator rescue.

"The part I played," Orsatti recalled for the 2003 documentary *Hell Under Water, Fire in the Sky*, "called for a six-foot-four,

---

170 *"Firestarter* Went as far as Possible for Its Explosive Special Effects," Anthony Orlando, Slashfilm.com (updated: https://www.slashfilm.com/862175/firestarter-went-as-practical-as-possible-for-its-explosive-special-effects/)
171 Noel Murray, *The Dissolve*, June 12, 2014.
172 Correspondence with author, July 8, 2022.

blond, blue-eyed guy. You know McQueen's not gonna look up to anybody and they're not gonna have blues, and they're not gonna compete with him. I got the part, I'm on the set, I'm doing the job, and McQueen comes on his first day of work, and the first thing I hear out of his mouth is, 'Who's playing that part, the six-foot-four blond, blue-eyed guy?' 'Here, sir,' and I shrunk down a little. He came up and he looked straight at me and said, 'oh, you're okay.' I was gonna get fired if I was six-foot-four, blond, blue-eyed. He wasn't gonna look up to anybody."

Orsatti told a slightly different version of that story to James Bacon just before the film opened. Bacon reported seeing Orsatti's stunt double hanging from the scenic elevator "fifty or more feet above an airbag held below by a dozen firemen. The stuntman let loose and dropped safely on the airbag." Ernie the actor couldn't forget his old profession. "That's a $400 stunt," he remarked. "As an actor, you don't get paid extra."[173] (It might have been that Orsatti got the close-ups with McQueen but, when it came time for him to let go, they cut to a stunt performer.)

Fire stunts are particularly hazardous because of the uncertain nature of fire even in the best circumstances. Early fire gags are said to have involved dousing the performer in rubbing alcohol which burned comparatively coolly and quickly, but also nearly invisibly. The more common practice was to wrap the stunt per-former in clothing made of non-flammable material, cover their skin with protective masks, run breathing apparatus under the faceplate, and get it over with as quickly as possible.

In the early 1980s special effects innovator Gary Zeller invent-ed a substance he called Zel-Jel.® Zel-Jel is a professional barrier gel that smears on like lotion and acts as a thermal shield against pyrotechnics. Zeller was given an Academy Award® for his work in 1989.

"I was always fascinated by movie actors asking me about fire," Zeller told producer Michael Lennick. "The [stunt people] would put on layers and layers of clothing. Dar Robinson in *Nighthawks*

---

173 James Bacon, "The Movie Army of Irwin Allen," *Los Angeles Herald-Examiner*, September 1, 1974.

(1981) wore a full-body burn suit. He was the first person I saw doing a fire gag, and he took a check out of his pocket and showed me what they paid him." When Zeller developed Zel-Jel, "we used it for the first time in *The Dead Zone* (1983) and then it found its way into the industry."[174]

Patented and now marketed "to the trade," it has been used by such well-known stunt performers, in addition to Robinson, as George Gibbs, Kenny Endoso, Terry Forrestal, Jery Hewitt, Alex Stevens, R.A. Rondell, Al Jones, Phil Chong, and Vic Armstrong and in such films (as listed on Zeller's website) as *Rambo, Cat's Eye, Firestarter, Scanners, Dawn of the Dead, Young Sherlock Holmes, Indiana Jones & the Temple of Doom, Deadly Force Silverado, Year of the Dragon, Planes, Trains & Automobiles, Taps, Altered States, Doctor Detroit, The Blob, Neighbors, Nighthawks, Nightmare on Elm Street, The Fly, Conan, Back to the Future*, and *Cape Fear*.[175] Its absence from *The Towering Inferno* is a matter of the production date.

Now, of course, CGI can produce flames but, as Teller says, audiences somehow know the difference. What cannot be faked is the expertise, athleticism, and dedication of the movies' stunt performers.

---

174 Interviewed by Michael Lennick for the Criterion disc *Scanners* (2014).

175 http://www.zeller-int.com/categories/fireret/zeljel.htm

Chapter 11 Sidebar: Stunt Performers

The stunt performers who worked on *The Towering Inferno* were: Phil Adams, M. James Arnett, Bruce Paul Barbour, Lightning Bear, Cody Bearpaw, Buff Brady, Tony Brubaker, Richard E. Butler, Hank Calia, Mickey Caruso, Roydon Clark, Erik Cord, Everett Creach, Roger Creed, Paula Crist, Dick Crockett, Howard Curtis, Vince Deadrick, Sr., Paula Dell, Dick Dial, Nick Dimitri, Bennie E. Dobbins, Larry Duran, Bud Ekins, Gary Epper, Jeannie Epper, Stephanie Epper, Tony Epper, Diamond Farnsworth, Lila Finn, George Fisher, James W. Gavin, Mickey Gilbert, Sandra Lee Gimpell, Orwin C. Harvey, Eddie Hice, Larry Holt (doubling Paul Newman), Loren James (doubling Steve McQueen), Mike Johnson (doubling Robert Wagner), Mike Johnson, Kevin N. Johnson, John Landis, Gene LeBell, Julius LeFlore, Fred Lerner, Lars Lundgren, Denver Mattson, John Hugh McKnight, Troy Melton, John Moio, Minor Mustain, John Nowak, Doug O'Dell, Ernie F Orsatti, Frank Orsatti, Regine Parton, Regis Parton, Victor Paul, Gil Perkins, Preston Peterson, Bobby Porter, Glenn Randall, Jr., Frank Reinhard, Robert Renegade Renneke (doubling Robert Wagner), Dar Robinson, Walter Robles, George Robotham, Thomas Rosales, Jr., Wally Rose, Glynn Rubin, Russell Saunders, Fred Scheiwiller, David Sharpe, Rodell Sharpe, Felix Silla, Dean Smith, Shelley Snell, Marilyn Stader, Paul Stader, Peter Stader, Tom Steele, Bob Terhune, Jack Verbois, Richard Washington, Chuck Waters, Fred Waugh, George P. Wilbur, James Winburn, Bob Yerkes, Fred Zendar. Steve McQueen and Paul Newman are also credited with doing stunts.[176]

---

176 Yes, the stunt performer named John Landis is the same John Landis who would make his mark as a full-time director starting in 1978 with *Animal House* (in which he also did stunt work in a scene he cut from the finished film).

Chapter 12: A New Kind of Marketing

There was a time in America when, if a movie was advertised on TV, it had to be lousy. Nowadays if a movie *isn't* advertised on TV, you think the same thing. The times, marketing, and audience perceptions have changed to the point where today's big-budget studio releases are no longer mere movies but finely engineered, often impersonal, committee-honed entertainment juggernauts.

For decades, new films were distributed by a method called platforming; that is, they opened in a single prestigious theatre in each city, played for a week or two, and then—starting in the 1950s when suburbs were invented—opened in a limited number of regional houses. After that they would "go wide" by appearing for a week "at a theatre or drive-in near you." Then they would disappear until they were either re-released (which was rare) or sold to TV. At each stage, costly newspaper and radio advertising supported the engagements.

This changed in the fifties when movies began being advertised on television. It's hard to know when the first movie ad ran on a TV station—they were already widely advertised and promoted on radio—but television advertising took a long time to catch on because Hollywood deemed it The Enemy. And it was; in 1947, the first year of commercial television broadcasting in America,[177] the film industry sold ninety million tickets a week. By 1950, TV sets were everywhere and ticket sales had dropped to sixty million a week.[178] The antipathy was so fierce that some studios refused to allow television sets to appear in their movies or, if they did, the scene had to show the set being on the blink.

---

177 Robert L. Hilliard, *The Broadcast Century: A Biography of American Broadcasting*, Stoneham, Massachusetts: Butterworth-Heinemann, 1992.

178 Cobbett Steinberg, *Reel Facts: The Movie Book of Records*, updated edition, New York: Vintage Books, 1982.

A generation that grew up under the triple threat of comic books, movies, and television remembers that only certain kinds of movies were advertised on TV, and most of them seemed to star Steve Reeves. In 1958 the ever-savvy Joseph E. Levine—who, in those days, was driving a taxi cab in Boston and had a tiny second-floor office called Embassy Pictures staffed by his brother, Morris—heard of an Italian muscleman picture called *Le fatiche di Ercole* (*The Labors of Hercules*) that had been turned down by all the major studios. He scraped together $120,000 and bought the epic's U.S. rights, dubbed it (more or less) into English, got Warner Bros. to ante $300,000 for the distribution rights and commit $1.25 million in advertising, more than producer Federici Teti had spent making the whole film.[179] Knowing it would be killed by word-of-mouth within days of its opening, he skipped the platforming stage and booked it into every available screen in each given territory. He started in July 1959 with 500 prints, moving them from one territory to another week by week just ahead of the scathing reviews. Levine himself said it was, "One of the worst pictures I ever saw, but I knew it had great appeal. There was a market for anything then." Thanks to his showmanship and guile, *Hercules* grossed $1 million in its first ten days and kept earning money for years.[180] This pattern became known as "saturation booking" and it was always supported by heavy TV advertising on local stations, which was cheap in those days.

Today the same system is used, only instead of $1.25 million the marketing budget for a big film can exceed $20 million. Before the arrival of streaming, it was not uncommon for a mega-budget studio release to open on several thousand screens at the same time, a far cry from the platforming that existed through the middle 1970s. (Today platforming is reserved largely for independent or special handling films.) Then, too, advertising and marketing have become far more sophisticated, and the first film to use

---

179 "*Hercules* Has 6,000 WB Dates Lined Up," *Weekly Variety*, July 15, 1959.

180 Rentals (returns to the studio) of between $4.7 and $5 million have been variously reported. "Joseph E. Levine, Movie Mogul Known for Flamboyance and Daring," *Santa Ana Orange County Register*, August 1, 1987.

modern sales techniques—techniques that changed the foundation of motion picture distribution—was *The Towering Inferno*.

The man behind the innovations was a soft-spoken Nebraskan named David M. Forbes.

Forbes had worked in publicity for MGM in the early 1970s when the fabled studio was still reeling from the damage wrought by its president, James T. Aubrey, who had ruled from 1969-1973. He was brought to Fox by Jonas Rosenfield, a savvy advertising-publicity executive who saw that he had worked with both the sales and advertising departments at Metro, a common-sense approach that was rare at other film companies where the sales and advertising departments were at odds (because sales collected the money while advertising spent it.).

"When I was at MGM nobody in the industry was really knowledgeable or adept at media," Forbes recounts. "The history had been that newspaper was the way you sold a movie and you supplemented it with this ridiculous waste of time on television. At the time they were still buying a lot of radio. When Jonas brought me over, I think somebody in the industry had oversold a movie using television, not really knowing what was going on, and they were looking for somebody who could sort this out."[181]

With a methodology that could rival that of Stanley Kubrick, Forbes broke out how many theatres were in each territory and how far the local broadcast television signals reached, then decided to book screens to fall within the umbrella of the signal rather than pick theatres first and buy the TV ads afterward.

"I spent some time working with [Jonas] and the sales department so that we could find enough theatres to completely saturate the territories and then be able to buy enough broadcast at low enough rates. Nobody really did it that way. We were figuring out how much per [rating] point you should be spending on average, what it would take to sell the movie and oversell the movie. The point was to force the audience to see the movie in the first week because then they'd realize the movies weren't really very

---

181 Author interview

good. For the most part these were action movies that were not gonna get reviews and not good word of mouth."

In a sense, it was Joe Levine's saturation booking all over again, only advertised not with a blunderbuss but with a precision rifle. "What I was saying was that we needed to get this number of rating points targeted to this specific audience over this period of time, and it has to build at this level. Then you open the movie in as many theatres as possible so you entice enough people to go that you make money, and then it dwindles out and you don't spend much money after that. You spend a little the second weekend advertising. That was the idea."

Forbes tested his theory with the romantic-action picture *Dirty Mary, Crazy Larry* opening May 17, 1974, "and it turned out to be a huge success. Which meant that they were going to find as many movies as possible to do this with. The truth was that we went through the first summer doing this very successfully, but by the end of that first summer every other studio was doing it and the audience had figured out that just because there's a lot of TV advertising doesn't mean the movie's good."

In other words, it was back to the days *Hercules*. The difference this time was that the marketing was more efficient so that, when a good movie came along, it could be targeted to reach the audience that could best appreciate it and would play at enough theatres to make money as soon as possible.

Thus began the now-controversial but prevailing wisdom that a movie has to open big on a Friday or it's dead by Monday.

"It worked," Forbes concludes. "What it did was force Fox to recognize the value of a multi-level media campaign and how to be more sophisticated. I was doing seminars in demographics and media buying at the studio to help people understand how it worked. It was the beginning of more modern media buying. We weren't the only ones trying to figure it out, but because I didn't know any better, I was probably more sophisticated than anybody else was."

In addition to boking theatres for *The Towering Inferno* to fall within broadcast umbrellas, Forbes also assembled a team of special publicists who covered the country territory by territory setting up promotions, visiting exhibitors, touring celebrities, and monitoring press screenings. They (we) worked in association with the Fox studio and field publicity staff who were busy handling all of the company's other films, not just Irwin Allen's. Tie-ins were made with fire departments in the major cities who by and large endorsed the film's call for greater fire prevention programs. Everything culminated on December 14, 1974 when *The Towering Inferno* opened in every major American city and pulled in $2,323,621 over its first weekend.

It was a hit.

After leaving Fox, Forbes headed Orion Pictures for a time, dabbled in independent producing, and ultimately founded the Accidental Wine Company with his son, Micah, his daughter Kelly, and marketing director Janice C. Lee. The company buys up "blemished but unbroken bottles" in cases of wine that may otherwise be damaged between vintner and retailer, or where the labels may have been damaged or the brand name didn't catch on.[182] Like the movies, wine must be opened properly, but at least the good ones don't spoil after the first weekend. (https://www.accidentalwine.com/)

---

182 Unsigned article, Associated Press, January 7, 2010.

Chapter 13: Fate vs. Justice

Why does disaster strike? Is it payback for sins or just Fate playing whoopee?

Thornton Wilder's short 1927 novel *The Bridge of San Luis Rey* considered that timeless, troubling question. His book is a haunting meditation on fate that tells of five people who plunge to their deaths when a rope bridge in Peru gives way, and the narrative follows the factual and spiritual investigation of the monk Brother Juniper to try to explain what brought those five people to their doom. It won the Pulitzer prize in 1928 and has been assigned reading for thousands of high school students ever since. It was also turned into three theatrical films, a TV movie, an opera, and a play for puppets, all of them essentially coming to the same conclusion as Brother Juniper: who knows the answer to such questions?

There are parallels that can be drawn between Wilder's novel and disaster films, but they depend on the degree to which we can learn about—and therefore identify with—the characters.

Given the commercial requirements of casting, it's rare to find a group jeopardy film whose jeopardized group is more than a gaggle of stereotypes. While screenwriter Stirling Silliphant alluded to this when he called *The Towering Inferno* characters stereotypes, he also explained (as with Steve McQueen's lisp) that it's the screenwriter's job to adjust dialogue and details once a particular actor is cast for a specific role. Thanks to his skill and the consideration of Fox, Warners, and Irwin Allen to accord the film a longer than usual running time, the Brother Junipers sitting in the audience have a lot more to work with in asking what brought the major characters to the top of the Glass Tower on the night of its simultaneous opening and closing. Here are sketches of the principal characters as specifically defined in the screenplay, where such descriptions are present, and as elucidated by the skilled performers playing them:

Doug Roberts (named "Craig Wilson" in the script) is described as "mid-thirties, blue-jeaned, face with a three-day stubble, a happy-looking cat, eyes bright and aware." At the time, Paul Newman was 49 and takes a shave in the story ten pages later. An architect, Roberts has been decompressing in Montana after having spent the last however-long supervising construction of the Glass Tower which he designed for his friend and employer, James Duncan. He knows every inch of the building intimately, which is how he quickly sees that his specifications for construction materials have been changed. He has also had a long-term relationship with journalist Susan Thompson whom he wants to marry and move with her to Montana, apparently having no notion of the Women's Movement or, to look at it more positively, simply according her the respect to be herself. Interestingly, although he is played by movie star Paul Newman, Roberts is not drawn as an action hero. His character arc in the course of the story will be that he rises to the occasion, largely at the goading of (or, more likely, in competition with) fire chief Mike O'Hallorhan. In retrospect, he probably should have stayed on the job rather than hie off to the hills, and this may inform the guilt he feels for leaving responsibility in the hands of people whom he may not have known were having financial problems, but undoubtedly should have.

Mike O'Hallorhan: With his introductory scene (he lives on a houseboat with his son, Mike Jr., and pregnant wife, Dorothy) cut, his present entrance is his arrival at the scene of the fire. "The Battalion Commander's car rolls in," the script reports, "O'Hallorhan boils out. He's wearing a white, short-sleeved shirt, black tie, uniform trousers–and his badge." No age is specified for the Chief, but Steve McQueen was 44. O'Hallorhan is the single major character in the film who is without any kind of guilt for the fire, which is ultimately why McQueen wanted to play the part. He is strictly by-the-book, keeping any hectoring to himself until the very end. He is all business, a solid leader as evinced not only by the instructions he barks to his crews but in his sensitive handling of a young firefighter who is afraid to rappel. Only when he is offered the chance to "volunteer" to drop to the roof of the tower to set charges that will blow up the water tanks does he act like a movie hero, and even then it's a pragmatic decision.

James Duncan: He is "fifty-three, one of the world's richest men, a tough-up-from-the-streets developer-builder. Even with his business suit pummeled by the wind [atop the Tower waiting for Roberts' 'copter to land], he gives off an aura of success and power. He appears–at the moment–to be literally and figuratively on top of the world." William Holden was a weathered 66 when he played Duncan who, we learn along the way, is not above bribing with a case of rare wine the Senator who heads the committee that approves his urban renewal plans, or for leaning on his son-on-law to cut corners on the construction rather than cut floors on the building. Greedy for the contract that will give him the urban renewal commission (for which he tries to inveigle Roberts out of retirement), he comes to realize that the fire is essentially his fault, yet–and this is Hollywood at work–William Holden himself is such a likable, upright guy that the audience has a hard time pointing its finger at him. He even announces to people waiting for rescue that he will be the last to go. Had Burt Lancaster taken the role, as was originally offered, he might have made the duplicity more believable, adding an undercurrent of self-awareness to the interpretation.

Susan Thompson: Devoid of physical description save for one line of dialogue ("Why did I have to be born short-wasted?"), Susan is a role in search of a backstory. She is a newspaper reporter who has been offered a position as managing editor and has to make a choice between Roberts and Pulitzer, so to speak, and she favors Pulitzer. Had she not been played by

Faye Dunaway, 33 when *Inferno* was shot, she would have been disposable. Dunaway had just come off *The Three/Four Musketeers*, in which she played a villainess, and *Chinatown*, in which she played a woman with a secret, and was heading into *Network* and *Three Days of the Condor*, so perhaps it's best to think of Susan as a rest stop rather than a stepping stone. Of note is that, despite being a journalist worthy of a promotion to managing editor, Susan does no reporting in the course of the film and never even resolves to tell the whole story once the danger is over. What a shame that the scene with Patty (Susan Blakely), in which the two women discuss the pros and cons of romance, was cut from the final release. It might have given both actresses something more to do.

Harlee Claiborne: Called "a distinguished-looking gentleman, late forties, a charmer, well-dressed," he is played by 75-year-old Fred Astaire. Harlee is a con man who has lost the will to con and is down to his last fifty-five cents (even though he has had enough to rent a tux, pay a photocopier, and keep an apartment in the Tower's ninety-fifth floor). He is apparently there at the invitation of Lisolette Mueller, his neighbor, whom he intends to swindle with worthless stock certificates. As he develops true feeling for her, he decides to come clean about himself, but tragedy gets in the way. He displays a modicum of heroism by using his rented jacket to cover the corpse of a man who dies in flames from an elevator, and otherwise charms his way through the disaster. Astonishingly, Astaire was nominated for his only Academy Award® for *The Towering Inferno*, perhaps his weakest and least characteristic performance.

Lisolette Mueller: The apple of Harlee Claiborne's jaundiced eye, or perhaps only his swindler's mark, she is a rich widow who dabbles in art. She is "also in her late fifties, with a soft, compassionate quality." Jones, then 56, plays Lisolette as a secure woman who loves children while apparently having none of her own, has a cat, and can summon great outer and inner strength to rise to the occasion by shinnying down a collapsed stairwell. The extent of her courage is rewarded when she is given a place in the last descent of the scenic elevator "because she saved the children" from a burning apartment. Alas, it is all for naught, because she is thrown from the scenic elevator when an explosion rips it off its tracks.

Patty Duncan Simmons: The daughter of builder James Duncan, Patty fell for Roger Simmons who also fell for her, but only intermittently. Played sweetly and honestly by Susan Blakely (27 and making only her fourth film), she remains in love with Roger even as he reveals his duplicity and cowardice. Patty also loves her father despite his confession that he is the cause of the Glass Tower tragedy. Blakely wanted to play her as a dowdy rich girl who had such a low self-image that she would accept a philandering husband, thoughtfully developing her character far beyond her function in the story. A true innocent, Patty may have erred in judging husbands and forgiving her father too easily, but her honesty among the sordid collection of characters is refreshing.

Roger Simmons: Although his corner-cutting is blamed for igniting the fire, he tries to dodge his responsibility when challenged by the architect, saying, "Everything I did is strictly up to Code!" In expanding his culpability beyond being a mere movie villain and implying that every municipality in the world has outdated fire safety codes, Roger becomes a kind of perverse oracle. Roger "exudes Eastern Establishment, clothes, manner, attitudes." He is played by 40-year-old Richard Chamberlain with a level of self-assurance that only a character's self-justification can inspire. But just in case anyone should think he is being altruistic, he first tries to escape down the stairs and later scuttles the breeches buoy, falling to his deserved death. Nevertheless, Patty will mourn him.

"He was such a jerk," Chamberlain said, "which was fun. It's fun to play a jerk, but I think I let on too early in the performance that he was not to be trusted. I think I should have played him like a hero, like a junior Paul Newman. And then it comes out that he's the one who, in league with his father-in-law, by the way, pretty much destroyed the building. And then he elbowed old ladies out of the way when he wanted to go to the saving swing out of the top floor and then, of course, fell to his death, which was highly deserved."[183]

Harry Jernigan: Specified in the script as "a rugged-looking black in his early thirties, Head of Security," he is played by O. J. Simpson, then 28 and currently running back with the Buffalo Bills. Jernigan and Chief O'Hallorhan are the only two characters who truly know their jobs. In addition to calling in the fire, Jernigan also helps rescue children and Lisolette's cat. He is guiltless.

Senator Gary Parker: As lubricious as they come, he is played by suave actor Robert Vaughn, then 43. The head of the Congressional urban renewal committee, Parker is in the pocket of Duncan, who provides him with a case of rare wine in certain belief that the multi-million-dollar construction contract will be his. Parker is a survivor, even over the bodies of others, as he suggests that he and Duncan try the stairwell, only to find it blocked. In the end he jumps aboard the over-loaded breeches buoy with the expected gravitational results.

Dan Bigelow: James Duncan's polished public relations man. The script describes his crowded desk and jammed office but it doesn't describe him. As Bigelow, Robert Wagner looks younger than his 45 years. He plays it slick but not sickeningly slick and, after dispatching his duties welcoming the media, joins his secretary, Lorrie, with whom he is having an illicit affair, although it's never clear what's illicit about it because neither of them is portrayed as married. Perhaps it's a no-mixing corporate employee policy that they're breaking. But he truly loves her; he even lies

---

183 Interviewed in *Pioneers of Television*, director Steven J,. Boettcher. https://www.youtube.com/watch?v=RJjHRZrqj7k

to her that help is on the way so he can delay as long as possible her realization that she is doomed. Screenwriter Silliphant started out in movie publicity and it's possible that he wanted to make a hero out of the public relations guy for old time's sake.

Lorrie: The only character with no discoverable last name, Lorrie is Dan Bigelow's secretary who is revealed as much more than that. Played by Susan Flannery, 36, Lorrie is clearly executive material but is caught in a man's world; we know this because she takes off her glasses to appear more attractive. Her death by fire is gruesome. Her ordeal shows the audience that flames are not the only danger in a fire. Her slow suffocation is easily the most personal and disturbing in the film because it is prolonged as she chokes on smoke before being blown out the window in an air-fueled fireball.

If there is anything to be learned from *The Towering Inferno* it is that Justice is just as fickle as Fate. How is it just when seven main characters (Roberts, O'Hallorhan, Thompson, Duncan, Cathy, Jernigan, and Claiborne) survive while five (Lisolette, Roger, Parker, Bigelow, and Lorrie) do not? Of the dead, four have varying levels of guilt: one crook/possible adulterer (Simmons), one bribed politician (Parker), and two office dalliers (Bigelow and Lorrie); and one (Lisolette) has none. Significantly, Lisolette's is the only death for which anyone (Claiborne) is seen to mourn. Of the seven who live to tell their tale, one is charmingly guilty (Duncan), one has reformed (Claiborne), one is a naïf (Patty), one is a career woman who may or may not abandon her career for love (Susan), one started but neglected to finish his job (Roberts the architect), and two are without sin (O'Hallorhan and Jernigan[184]).

In a world where not even star billing can guarantee survival and justice is fickle at best, one is left trying to untangle the intricacies of Fate in *The Towering Inferno*. In Hollywood, this is a fool's errand. Whether it's a 138-story skyscraper matted into the

---

184 O.J.'s guilt comes later, but that's another story.

San Francisco skyline or a rope footbridge spanning a chasm in Peru, the only explanation is what makes for a better story, not what tells a greater truth.

Chapter 14: Fear of Fire: How America Took Notice

The Towering Inferno begins boldly and proudly with the onscreen title card, "To those who give their lives so that others might live—To the fire fighters of the world—This picture is gratefully dedicated." In the end credits, several participating and advising fire companies are also thanked and acknowledged.[185]

Like New York Mayor Fiorello LaGuardia and Boston "Pops" conductor Arthur Fiedler, both of whom were known to chase fire engines, Irwin Allen was a kid when it came to firemen. "It was wonderful becoming a fire chief in seventy-three countries throughout the world," he told an interviewer. "It was nice that fire chiefs throughout the world thought that the single greatest effort ever made in history for fire prevention was the production of the motion picture *The Towering Inferno*."[186]

The film did indeed spark a national discussion of high-rise fire safety, not only for what it showed but for what it said, and not just about fire dangers but the compromises that are made in building construction. "Let's put it this way," says Roger Simmons, the son-in-law who cut corners to save money, "everything I did is strictly up to code."

"Not good enough," responds the architect. "What the hell do the people who set up the Code know about our problems?"

The gap between fire codes and modern building construction is a message throughout the film, culminating in O'Hallorhan lecturing Roberts, "It'll happen again. One of these days ten thousand people are going to die in one of these skyscrapers."

---

185 One of the benefits of being on the publicity team for the film was that the author became an honorary member of the New York State Professional Fire Fighters Association (IAFF affiliated with the AFL-CIO).

186 Canned PR interview, *The Towering Inferno* 2003 DVD special features. A little exaggerated, perhaps.

Additional lines ("You going to fight fourteen thousand separate building codes in this country? Forget it! As long as some people care more about property–and saving a buck–than they do about other people") were cut, perhaps because they were too cynical, or perhaps because Steve McQueen didn't want to be a Cassandra. But the point was made.

Another important matter was introduced between O'Hallorhan and Jernigan when the security man advises him not to worry because business tenants had safely left the building. "I'm talking about who they are, not where they are," the fire chief says. "You got any silk importers? When silk burns, it gives off cyanide gas. You got any sports goods manufacturers? Table-tennis balls give off toxic gases. Want me to go down the line?"

Driving home the challenges to rescue, O'Hallorhan, in the film, says, "You know damn well that above the tenth floor there's no sure way we can fight these fires." When the scene was shot, the technical advisors advised them to change "tenth" to "seventh."

Granted, *The Towering Inferno* wasn't designed as a fire safety film and Steve McQueen didn't want to be saddled with being the messenger. From the danger of a ceiling fire, smoke asphyxiation, heat inhalation, elevators homing to the fire floor, flash fires, gas main explosions, and making sure a door is cool before opening it, it's abundantly apparent from the action itself that high rise fires are disasters waiting to happen. The final shot of the Glass Tower itself—structurally intact despite the deaths of nearly two hundred people who were inside it—says more about society's concern for the value of property than the value of human life.[187]

It must be said that building codes, materials, and safety standards have improved since 1974 (see Afterword). How real a danger is fire today? Like a cat, fire is something than Mankind thinks he has tamed, but never really has, and the moment he dares to think he has, fire disobeys him and does what it wants.

---

187   This point of structural integrity begs comparison with the collapse of the twin towers on 9/11. That is outside the scope of this book, but it is hereby noted.

When *The Towering Inferno* was released it not only entertained millions of people, it inspired them to look at the safety of their own homes and offices and, more than that, to demand upgrades in building codes on the city and state levels.

Allen knew he was poking the bear when he set out to make his epic, and the bear—namely, the building industry—did not take it kindly. "Several attempts were made to stop us from going ahead with the film," he told Gordon Gow in *Films and Filming*, "because it did say that high-rise buildings were all fire traps. It did say that loss of life was unnecessary. And in eleven countries throughout the world where the picture has been shown, legislation is undergoing a rethinking to try to put an end to this suicidal nonsense of people living and working in fire traps."[188]

The point was made graphically as *The Towering Inferno* readied to roll when, on February 1, 1974, fire broke out in the Joelma Building in Sao Paulo, Brazil killing 179 people. It is still the worst skyscraper fire after the World Trade Centers on September 11, 2001.

"Of course, the fire departments love us for making the picture," Allen went on. "The insurance companies adore us. And I would say that somewhere between eighty-five and ninety percent of the architects go along with us. The people who are distressed by us—well, I think *hate* would be the milder of the words that could be used for what they feel about us—are the builders, the real estate lobbies, the construction companies. Because they knew they're doing a bad thing, and they don't seem to have too much choice because it would cost them millions of dollars more than they're already spending in most instances to build a proper building with proper safety."[189]

Much has changed. At the time, some codes seemed designed to protect the building but not the people in it. Efficient evacuation capabilities are now stressed as the best way to survive a building fire. Yet it matters little how safe a structure is if the people inside it don't follow simple rules. Danger is never more

---

188   Gordon Gow, "Catastrophe: Irwin Allen," *Films and Filming*, September, 1975.
189   ibid

than a match or lighter away, according to the National Fire Protection Association (www.nfpa.org):[190]

- The prime days for home fires are Thanksgiving, Christmas, and New Year's. Kitchen fires, candle fires, Christmas tree fires, and electrical shorts on holiday decorations cause thousands of fires each year.
- A fire department in the United States responds to a fire somewhere every 23 seconds.
- Fire departments responded to an estimated average of 46,700 home fires involving electrical failure or malfunction each year in 2015–2019.
- Approximately 25 percent of home fires occur overnight during hours of sleep.
- Poverty is a factor in fire safety and death. Studies going back decades show that family stability, percentage of owner occupied vs. rented homes, and number of people under a single roof are risks in fire, as are people living in older or vacant homes and whether they can speak English.
- The five year period between 2015-2019 covered by the NFPA report saw 2,620 civilian deaths and 11,070 injuries in home fires.
- According to a government study by FEMA,[191] between 2010 and 2019 there was an average of 3,400 fire deaths each year in the U.S. or roughly eleven percent per million people.

After the film's release there were, as anticipated, those who disputed its accuracy. The United States Gypsum Company[192] in their trade publication *Business of Building* politely coun-

---

190 Statistics adapted from NFPA report: https://www.nfpa.org/News-and-Research/Data-research-and-tools/US-Fire-Problem/Intentional-fires

191 https://www.usfa.fema.gov/data/statistics/fire_death_rates.html

192 William D. Leavitt, "Creating a Hotbed of Controversy," *Business of Building*, United States Gypsum Company (undated, perhaps spring 1975), https://www.awci.org/cd/pdfs/7506_b.pdf

tered that, while the film was "entertainment at its best, creative license does not permit gross exaggeration of facts to achieve box office results." The company allowed that there were "good points made," but said that there were also a number of errors:

- Twenty or more explosions, ripping out the exterior walls, stairwells and service core of the building are shown in the movie but not explained.
- In one of the books and the movie, the architect was sent away while the shenanigans in material substitution were going on, The architect should not only approve material substitutions, but he should also check contractors for correct installations.
- The exterior concrete wall, reinforced with steel rods, should hold up, aided by the three interior walls.
- Fire is not likely to spread in an elevator or mechanical shaft. Fire-rated partitions in these areas resist passage of flame, and inside a shaft there is almost nothing to burn.
- It is unheard of for manufacturing or warehousing facilities to be located in high-rise buildings.
- The irony of the movie and the books is that they pick on one of the safest of all types of construction, the high-rise building.

Allen's response to such attacks was to turn them into publicity. "We must have done something right," he told columnist Cecil Smith, "because complaints from the insurance underwriters and the building industry are deafening. But," he continued, "I don't do message pictures. I do movies for entertainment and to make money so I can make more movies. But *Inferno* gets across the message that fireproof buildings are a joke, that the dangers in those skyscrapers is terrifying, and I'm glad."[193]

---

193 Cecil Smith, "Disaster Master Launches Grand Slam," *Los Angeles Times*, February 14, 1975.

He also said, "It's become a message movie although it was not intended to be one. Nevertheless, I'm glad if we can bring this horrendous situation to the public's attention."[194]

One aspect of the two source books that the film avoids entirely is the subject of arson. The National Fire Protection Association says in their 2021 report that fire departments responded to 52,260 intentionally set fires over a five year period between 2014 and 2018 that resulted in as many as 400 civilian deaths, 950 civilian injuries, and $815 million in direct property damage each year. People playing with fire accounted for over 50,000 fires.[195]

What is the human fascination with fire?

The clinical word for the desire to set fires is *pyromania*. A 2010 National Institutes of Health report[196] surveyed 43,000 adults during the 2001-2002 period. The interviewers paid personal visits to the households and evaluated their subjects on matters such as mood, drug abuse, anxiety, or personality disorders. They concluded that the risk "of lifetime fire setting in the U.S. population was. . .white, older than thirty years of age, never married, U.S.-born and with a yearly income over $70,000." The researchers concluded that fire setting was part of a syndrome rather than a one-off condition.

Other researches have called pyromania an "impulse control disorder." "While arson is typically used to burn things down in order to receive gain of some sort—ranging from monetary to personal," writes the Thriveworks staff from Boston Counseling Therapy, "pyromaniacs feel the urge to burn things in order to instantly receive pleasure or relief." There also needs to be more than one instance of fire setting to qualify as a pyromaniac.[197]

---

194   Gordon Gow, op cit.

195   https://www.nfpa.org/News-and-Research/Data-research-and-tools/US-Fire-Problem/Intentional-fires

196   https://www.ncbi.nlm.nih.gov/pmc/articles/PMC2950908/

197   "Pyromania Therapy Facts and Fictions," Boston Counseling Cambridge Therapy, August 30, 2018. (https://thriveboston.com/counseling/pyromania-therapy-facts-and-fictions/)

In *The Tower*, the disgruntled metal worker John Connors plants a bomb that triggers the fire. In *The Glass Inferno* the igniting culprit is a depressed mall business owner. Neither is a pyromaniac; their crime is arson, although faulty building construction exacerbates their deeds. *The Towering Inferno*, however, stays singly with compromised building codes, placing the guilt squarely on the people who build them higher without making them safer. This choice makes the story more relatable to the public than a lone arsonist or a pyromaniac. And it worked.

Whether it was *The Towering Inferno* that made people sit up, the natural advance of research and development by the construction industry, or a combination of both, safety conditions have indeed improved in the decades since its release. But it still comes down to the human element, and Smokey the Bear is long gone.

NOTE: See Afterword for a commentary from former Los Angeles Fire Chief Brian Cummings for a current appraisal of fire codes and survival efforts.

Chapter 15: The Failure of Success

Three years after *The Towering Inferno* was released, an interviewer asked Irwin Allen to list the rewards of movie making. He said, "First comes the money. Second, the money. Third. . .." Then he paused, smiled genuinely, and resumed, "In fact, there are a number of rewards and, cumulatively, they do come up to the money. It was marvelous getting an Academy Award® nomination for the picture. So there are any number of things including, in the action sequences, directing Steve McQueen and Paul Newman and William Holden and Faye Dunaway and Fred Astaire and Jennifer Jones and Richard Chamberlain and all the marvelous people that we cast in the show. There are endless rewards and, happily, they never seem to stop. The making of new pictures are all related back to the success of *The Towering Inferno*. I think that kind of sums up the different rewards." He paused again, then added, "And, of course, last of all, there's the money."[198]

Truth be told, Allen would have made movies for free. He loved them so. But he also knew that he had a reputation. "I'm a difficult fellow to work for," he admitted, then pulled back, "not really, but I pretend to be—and I'm a perfectionist. I do believe that this is an art form and should be treated as such. And, as you can see here in this room, you're sitting in the so-called Irwin Allen Think Tank. All projects start here. They all start visually, or with doing a visualization, of an idea, whether it's from a bestseller or an original idea, how is it going to look on the screen? The quickest and easiest way to find out is to have these remarkable artists that work for our operation translate to pictures that which the writer has put into words—the old Chinese proverb of a picture being worth ten

---

198   Interview bites, 2006 DVD special features

thousand words. We quickly can tell, based on these pictures, how to budget it, how to plan it, what's gonna be involved, the shooting time, the schedules, the thousands of requirements that may be necessary by way of props and sets and so on. Starting a picture starts with a picture. Say, that was rather clever."[199]

His last comment, self-congratulatory as it was, puts the previous comment in perspective. Irwin Allen was not a humble man. "He was like, in some respects, a bull in a china shop," said Don Kopaloff, an agent who had dealings with Allen during good times and bad. "He was Hollywood all the way. No matter where he went, he had to be first class. There were limos everywhere. And to a lot of the younger executives in Hollywood, the young people who were just starting to come forward—don't forget, this was the time when the old guard was on its way out and the new guard was coming in—they didn't take him seriously."[200]

Apparently "first class" applied when the studio was picking up the tab but not when Irwin himself was on the line. "He was the cheapest man in the world," said Stella Stevens, who co-starred in *The Poseidon Adventure*. "One day he invited me to lunch and I said, 'oh, that's great, the producer is taking me to lunch.' He picked me up in his cream-colored Rolls-Royce and he took me to Jack-in-the-Box drive-in. And I said, 'I don't eat meat. What are you doing here?' 'Oh, this is my favorite, you're gonna love it!' I said, 'No, I'm not gonna love it, I'm not gonna eat it. I don't eat meat. I'm sorry.' So I think I didn't eat that day. I said, 'Why did he do that? Was it a joke?' I came to find out from his wife later that it was his favorite restaurant. It was a high honor for him to take me there, and I had spurned it and probably crushed him. He never invited me again for lunch."[201]

Then there was his hair which, if it was not a toupee, looked like one.[202] "It was combed in a way, an incredibly complicated manner," recalled Richard Chamberlain, "so that, at any distance,

---

199 ibid
200 Interviewed in *Fire in the Sky, Hell Under Water*, 2003 Nobles Gate, Ltd.
201 "The Great Producer" featurette, 2003 special features *The Towering Inferno* DVD, produced in association with Creative Domain.
202 He began losing his hair in his twenties as can be seen in old photographs.

it looked like he had an abundant, full head of hair. But once you got up closer you could see all this weave intertwining. It must have taken hours and hours in the morning to do. I remember, occasionally, walking up behind him when he was directing and I would try to figure out what he had done and he always, always knew, he would always turn around the instant you gave his hair that kind of focus. He had a kind of hair radar."[203]

Recalls David Forbes, the studio's marketing expert, when it came to meetings, Allen "needed to be the one talking. A lot of the guys at Fox at the time were talkers and that was not what worked for him." And he had another peccadillo that hit Forbes on their first meeting. "We go to Irwin's office. You come into the room and I think everybody but me knew that Irwin was a germophobe. I shook hands with him, And then Irwin left the room. At the time he did not have a bathroom in his office, so he went back from the conference room into his office and then out another door so he could go out to the restroom and wash his hands. He had a bungalow but I guess it was the whole building. Then he comes back for the meeting. That's how I learned that you don't shake hands. There is no connection. I would see this in other meetings that I had with him later. People would come in and shake his hand and he would have to leave and come back before the meeting could start. Way after the fact, when he was at Warners, I went to have lunch with him just to stay in touch, and I had completely forgotten about the hygiene thing. We were at the Warners dining room. Bread came to the table. At some point I put my hand in there and took a piece of bread and, moments later, Irwin said to the waiter, 'could you bring me another basket of bread?' Oh shit, I forgot about that."[204]

After *Inferno* hit a home run, Allen took a victory lap at Fox. Rather than produce something else for theatres, however, he chose to sign what he called a "$3 million grand slam" with Twentieth Century-Fox Television for three pictures at $1 million each.

---

203 "The Great Producer" featurette, 2003 special features *The Towering Inferno* DVD, produced in association with Creative Domain. It was a combination hair weave and toupee. Trust me. I saw it in person.

204 Author interview January 17, 2022

"I spent two years and $14,733,000 making *The Towering Inferno*," he told the *Los Angeles Times*. "Twelve stars. Daily calls for 300 stunt people—the biggest calls for stunt people in history. It was like staging World War Five. The movie was more work and more fun than anything I ever did. But I missed television. Can you believe it? There's a hysteria and excitement in television that exists nowhere else in show business. After Inferno opened the networks were all after me to do something for them. I decided to try for a million dollar grand slam! A show for each network, each to cost $1 million. They went for it."[205] Allen at the time was just shy of his sixtieth birthday.

The first picture in his TV three-course dinner was *Adventures of the Queen* for CBS. To be shot aboard the drydocked Queen Mary, as was *Poseidon*, it was a back-door pilot in which a bomb is hidden aboard the luxury liner and the man who put it there wants $20 million ransom.[206] Obviously it wouldn't go off or else the rest of the series would have to be set in lifeboats. And speaking of *Poseidon*, Allen leased it to ABC-TV for one showing in the fall of 1974 for $3.3 million and then locked it away in the Fox vaults with plans for a major reissue. (It never happened; home video intervened.)

His other two TV productions were to be *The Swiss Family Robinson* (1975) for ABC (going back to the original inspiration of *Lost in Space*) and *The Time Traveler* for NBC to be written by Stirling Silliphant. It was eventually made as *Time Travelers* (1976) written by Jackson Gillis from a story by Rod Serling and Allen himself, who was not credited.

The most important Irwin Allen production, however, was his February 15, 1975 marriage to Sheila Mathews. She was 46, he was 59 and it was the first marriage for each of them. Mathews had played the mayor's wife in *The Towering Inferno*, but it was as Irwin Allen's wife that she landed her major role. Mathews had been acting since a small role in 1962's remake of *State Fair*. That

---

205 Cecil Smith, "Disaster Master Launches Grand Slam," *Los Angeles Times*, February 14, 1975.

206 The plot is reminiscent of Richard Lester's 1974 thriller *Juggernaut* about bombs hidden aboard a luxury liner.

year she also appeared in Allen's *Five Weeks in a Balloon* and began a career in his other series and films, continuing with an episode of *Voyage to the Bottom of the Sea* in 1964, which may be when she and Allen started dating when she was 36 and he was 48. She made episodes of *Lost in Space, Land of the Giants, City Beneath the Sea* and non-Allen shows such as *The Waltons and FalconCrest.* Her acting career continued until 1990, primarily in television and frequently in her husband's productions.

For the Mathews-Allen marriage, the groom took over nearly the entire Beverly Wilshire Hotel, booked a thirty-five piece orchestra, covered the hotel's spacious ballroom (capacity 880 people) with flowers, and staged the ceremony himself, using what could only be called assistant directors posing as ushers in the back of the room linked by walkie-talkies for crowd control.

As much planning and preparation went into his wedding as he put into his films. Everybody who was Anybody in Hollywood was there from Susan Blakely to Groucho Marx.[207] The bride's white dress was designed by Paul Zastupnevich, Allen's favored film costume designer, had flowers by Jef of Broadway, was officiated by Superior Court judge Sam Greenfield, and carried a whispered price tag of $100,000.[208]

Life was not all sunny, however. Even as *The Towering Inferno* was breaking box office records around the world, Twentieth Century-Fox was suffering corporate change. With cash flowing into its coffers, diversification was the buzzword and the idea was floated at the executive level to acquire Marineland of the Pacific, a theme park where wild water animals were held captive and forced to perform for tourists.[209] Fox's partner in the gambit was the Hollywood Turf Club which owned and operated the Hollywood Park Race Track and had purchased Marineland from its original builders in 1972. The team asked Irwin Allen to apply his showmanship to this new endeavor.

207　James Bacon, "Dancing at their Wedding," *Los Angeles Herald-Examiner,* February 18, 1975.

208　*Los Angeles Herald-Examiner,* February 24, 1975.

209　*The Hollywood Reporter,* December 12, 1974.

"The problem is that Marineland was a one-time attraction," he correctly perceived. "You'd go, you'd feed the seals, and then you'd go back home and tell everyone that you'd fed the seals. What we're creating now is the kind of park that demands return visits."[210]

Thinking that Fox should have a theme park like Universal and Disney, Allen went to work proposing ambitious ideas for the eighty-seven acre Palos Verdes Peninsula Coast property that housed Marineland, only twenty-three acres of which were in use. The future, he said, would feature, for example, a *Voyage to the Bottom of the Sea* ride, but he was otherwise vague-to-silent about his plans. He did, however, commence a sixteen-day "Winter Wonderland" event beginning December 21, 1974 and running through the holidays to January 5, 1975. It boasted a Santa's Workshop, concerts by the Mitchell Boys Choir, and a skating rink doused in 1,000 tons of snow each day provided by immense ice machines.[211] They needed it; the Southern California temperature on opening day was 70 degrees. Then it got worse.

A month after the article appeared, another one ran in the *Los Angeles Times*, this one reporting that Marineland agreed to pay $10,000 in civil penalties and $5,000 in attorneys' fees after the state attorney general's office accused it of falsely promising children snow last Christmas. "The igloo was plastic, the giant Alpine snow slide was Fiberglas, the snow train ran through cotton on an asphalt walkway, and youngsters were not allowed to break snow over each other's heads as advertised," the A.G.'s civil suit claimed. Despite all advertisements, the article said, "snow-hungry children were given a single bucket of snow and told to throw snowballs from a wooden desk at stationary objects." The upshot was that Marineland would no longer promise snow.[212] Allen declined to reveal his own financial involvement in Marineland and it was never mentioned publicly again.

---

210 *Los Angeles Herald-Examiner*, February 24, 1975.

211 Todd Everett, "Marineland Today: A 20th Century Snow Job?" *Coast* magazine, March 1975.

212 "Snow Ads Bring Marineland Fine," *Los Angeles Times*, April 4, 1975.

In 1978 Fox sold the park to Hanna-Barbera Productions who struggled with it until 1987, at which time it was again sold, this time to Harcourt, Brace, Jovanovich which owned the Sea World franchise. They shut Marineland and shipped the surviving animals to Sea World San Diego.[213]

Undaunted, and focusing solely on screen entertainment, Allen announced a new three-picture deal with the studio, this time for theatrical features: *The Day the World Ended*, *The Poseidon Adventure II*, and *Circus*.[214] These new projects, he reminded, were in addition to *The Swarm*, currently being scripted by Stirling Silliphant from the Frank Schätzing bestseller, and *The Walter Syndrome*, being written by Richard Neeley from his novel. Unlike *The Day the World Ended* (with Nelson Giddings scripting), *The Poseidon Adventure II*, and *Circus* (Edward Anhalt writing), *Swarm* and *Walter* had no studio attachments. With *Circus*, which Allen announced would be made with the Ringling Bros. and Barnum & Bailey Circus, he was toying with producing it in Imax or 70mm 3-D. It was never made.[215]

Almost simultaneously (on July 21, 1975) Allen announced an agreement with Warner Bros. that he touted as "the largest production deal in motion picture history." Under its $100 million terms, Allen would deliver two pictures the size of *The Towering Inferno* and "oversee other films in the $4 to $6 million range."[216] Covering the same announcement, *The Hollywood Reporter*'s Ron Pennington noted that the contract was the biggest in the history of Warner Bros., that Allen would not necessarily produce and/or direct the films, and that his other productions could well

---

213 Jonathan Cohn, "1970s Disasters: Irwin Allen, Twentieth Century-Fox's Marineland of the Pacific, and Disaster Films," *Spectator*, Spring 2012.

214 Ron Pennington, *The Hollywood Reporter*, July 18, 1975.

215 In working with Ringling et al, Allen would have been walking ground already trod by Cecil B. DeMille, as noted earlier. Also—and this is just auctorial speculation—one of the young publicists working for Allen on his special *Inferno* PR unit to which the author also belonged was Karen Feld, the daughter of Kenneth Feld whose Feld Entertainment operated the Ringling Circus. Small world.

216 "Irwin Allen, Warners Sign Production Deal," *Los Angeles Times*, April 21, 1975.

go to any studio.[217] Lastly, Warners was going to give Allen and his staff an entire three-story building on their Burbank lot.[218]

Enriched by multiple production deals, a marriage, and a building with his name on it, Allen produced eighteen movies and one TV series over the next seventeen years. None of them equaled in grosses, reviews, or stature that his inflammatory blockbuster he had made in 1974. Two, alas, vie for his creative nadir: *The Swarm* (1978), which he directed as well as produced, and *When Time Ran Out* (1980). The first was based an alarmist but fact-based novel about the encroachment of African "killer bees" into the borders of the United States, supplanting European honeybees and angrily attacking humans and animals for no apparent reason. Allen commanded a major cast for this film including Michael Caine, Henry Fonda, Richard Chamberlain, Katharine Ross, and Olivia de Havilland—all if not most of them doing it for the payday.

"They put a load of bees above us one time," recalled Michael Caine, "me and Henry Fonda. There was all these bees up in the [soundstage] and the bee keeper was supposed to be keeping them up and then descend on us and the stunt people would take over. And as we were talking we both noticed little specs of black on our shirts. And we looked up and the bees were shitting on us. We didn't know it, but when the first reviews were in, then the critics did it."[219]

The budget, variously reported at between $11.5 million and $21 million, yielded a gross of only $7.7 million[220] that computes roughly to a return of $3.85 million which in all likelihood wouldn't have covered marketing costs. Was *The Swarm*'s buzz defused by competition like *Killer Bees* (1974), *The Savage Bees* (1976), and *The Bees* (1978)? Were bees not widely enough perceived as

---

217 Ron Pennington, "Allen Signs Two-Year-Contract with Warners," *The Hollywood Reporter*, July 21, 1975.

218 *The Hollywood Reporter*, September 30, 1975.

219 BBC *The One Show* interview May 19, 1991. https://www.youtube.com/watch?v=A6O4fEdBOU8

220 Lawrence Cohn, "All-Time Film rental Champs," *Variety*, October 15, 1990.

a threat?[221] Or was it simply a camp subject that wasn't treated in a campy enough manner; e.g., a film that took itself too seriously? It might even have been the endless routines by *Saturday Night Live*'s Not Ready for Primetime Players getting laughs by posing in striped jerseys, wings, and antennae as killer bees. Whatever the reason, the damage was done and the results were a slap in the face of the man who didn't know what went wrong.

What went wrong was that movies—indeed, all of America—was changing. The late 1970s saw the emergence of a concept called "lifestyle" in which the Me Generation was celebrating itself and developing a lack of empathy that would persist in American life and politics well into the next century. And if there's one thing that disaster films require, it's empathy.

That didn't occur to the people who financed and made *When Time Ran Out* (filmed under the title *The Day the World End-ed* after the book by Gordon Thomas and Max Morgan Witts). Allen produced and James Goldstone directed an all-star group of vacationers at a South Seas island resort who are threatened when a volcano erupts and a brave oil rigger risks his life to save them. Under the lucrative terms of his *Towering Inferno* contract, Paul Newman was obligated to do another picture for Allen and this turned out to be it. Rather than try to negotiate his way out, the honorable Newman bit his lip and soldiered on. His co-stars were Jacqueline Bissett, William Holden, Edward Albert, Darrell Larson, and a restless volcano.

When Time Ran Out has the dubious distinction of being scripted by two Oscar®-winning writers: Carl Foreman (after Nelson Giddings departed) who was then rewritten by Stirling Silliphant (*In the Heat of the Night*). "I was doing great with the first two, *Poseidon* and *Towering*," Silliphant blushed. "But the downward spiral was my getting involved in those two classic golden turkeys *The Swarm* and *When Time Ran Out*. I have never been able to bring myself to screen *When Time Ran Out*, so hor-rendous was the experience of being within a thousand miles of

---

221 Africanized honeybees (a.k.a. "killer bees") truly were a threat, not only to humans and other animals but to the bee industry.

it. What respect my sixteen-year-old son may or may not have got for me has, over the years, been in group jeopardy of fusing out because of my involvement with these final two gasps of the 'GJ genre.'"

Despite *The Swarm* and *When Time Ran Out* tanking, Irwin Allen's reputation as the Master of Disaster was safe, although the specialty itself was rapidly falling out of favor. For a while it was even rumored that journalists wishing to interview Allen had to promise not to mention those two films in his presence.

Many disaster/group jeopardy films followed *Poseidon*'s and *Inferno*'s successes but few were respected or effective. Two that stood out were Richard Lester's often screwy but unbearably tense *Juggernaut* and Joseph Sargent's relentlessly effective *The Taking of Pelham One-Two-Three*, both 1974. It should be noted, however, that neither was a true disaster film. *Juggernaut* involved a bomb on a cruise ship and *Pelham* a New York subway train held for ransom. The passengers on each vehicle were barely drawn, let alone featured. Neither involved Nature taking its toll on Man's arrogance.

Not looking at the competition, Allen himself continued producing with *Flood* (TV, 1976), *Fire* (TV, 1977), *Beyond the Poseidon Adventure* (1979), *The Night the Bridge Fell Down* (1980), and *Cave-in!* (1983), of which less said, the better. His one acknowledged success was a two-part, all-star television production of *Alice in Wonderland* adapted by Paul Zindel and directed by Harry Harris in 1985 for CBS. Allen gathered around him his stalwarts: Red Buttons, Roddy McDowall, Shelley Winters, Ernie Orsatti, Ernest Borgnine, costume designer Paul Zastupnevich, cinematographer Fred Koenekamp, production illustrator Joseph Musso, and stunt coordinator Paul Stader.

Always a movie fan, always optimistic, and always running at full throttle, Allen loved making movies. After a while, however, the public lost interest in the kind of films he made.

"He was one of a kind," recalled Stirling Silliphant. "He was a dear friend. He was often irascible, but never toward me, though he was endlessly demanding. Yes, he was vain. He could be arrogant—because he knew what he wanted, even if what he wanted was sometimes not the best choice. He lacked, I say with regret, the kind of sophisticated taste which would have let him produce a film like *Chariots of Fire*. But then, who knows, he MIGHT have been able to do that had he chosen. But he was a showman. He loved the circus. He loved prancing horses and gyrating clowns. But be stayed too long at the fair. He should have gone onward and upward after *The Towering Inferno*—sought new directions."[222]

"He was a frustrated director," said Jeff Bond, "and was given a certain amount of license by the studios, especially Fox, but when it got to be a very high profile, expensive movie like *The Poseidon Adventure* they did not trust him to direct it, and they did not trust him to direct *The Towering Inferno*. But when he made that deal and got Warner Bros. and Fox to work together, which was a brilliant piece of deal-making on his part, Warner Bros. then pursued him because he was literally Steven Spielberg in the first half of the 1970s. He was the guy making the special effects movies that were the biggest blockbusters that anybody had ever seen. Warner Bros. lured him over there and gave him a building and this incredible contract and all these projects he was going to do, but then he wound up directing them and they turned out terrible. He flamed out fast. By the time he made *The Swarm*, *Jaws* and *Star Wars* had taken over and he could not compete on that level even though he laid the groundwork for a lot of those films with his shows and movies. But his productions were still old Hollywood. He was a creature of the studio system and of glamor. He didn't understand why *Star Wars* was a hit because it didn't have any glamorous movie stars in it."[223]

"Irwin was like a little boy in a way," recalled Marta Kristen (*Lost in Space*). "He loved the explosions, he loved all the special effects, he loved action."[224]

---

222 *The Fingers of God, op cit*

223 Author interview June 15, 2022.

224 Interviewed in *The Fantasy Worlds of Irwin Allen*, Van Ness Films/SciFi Channel, 1995.

"He was a pioneer," said Lee Meriwether (*Land of the Giants*). "He was a man who always knew what was going on in all of his sets, all of his scripts, all of his writers, directors, even his casts. He was the consummate professional producer."[225]

From Jeff Bond, author of the book *The Fantasy Worlds of Irwin Allen*: "You get some sense that he was a young kid attracted to glamor and adventure and Hollywood provided it."[226]

"Irwin Allen had, famously, a carnival mentality," says Teller, "but with this vast level of skill and vast resources to draw from. He has really all the finest artists and designers around, working on making that movie work. You also learn something from it. You learn the rig by which firemen transport people out a building, in a little chair or by a cable. You actually *learn* something from that. You don't learn anything from *Earthquake*."[227]

"I found him fascinating," offers Susan Blakely. "Here I was just getting started, and he was a real Hollywood mogul type. Mike Frankovich was one of them as well. I remember Irwin Allen saying to me, after he had seen some of the first dailies, "Hey, kid, you're gonna be a big star, big star." It was like the cliché. He said it like an old-fashioned mogul. I loved his energy. He reminded me of New Yorkers. His taste wasn't exactly mine–I never saw any of those disaster movies–and I wouldn't have even been in this, and then it became this big commercial hit."[228]

A pulmonary condition forced Allen into semi-retirement in the 1980s, a work status that probably gave him more pain than his failing heart. He suffered a fatal heart attack at his and Sheila's $5.5 million[229] La Costa Beach, Malibu home on November 2, 1991 and was pronounced dead when he arrived at Santa Monica Hospital Medical Center.

Allen's funeral the next day at the Mount Sinai Memorial Park in Burbank drew 350 people including, according to the press

---

225 Interviewed in *The Fantasy Worlds of Irwin Allen*, Van Ness Films/SciFi Channel, 1995.

226 Author interview July 15, 2022.

227 Noel Murray, *The Dissolve*, June 12, 2014.

228 Author interview July 13, 2022

229 The house was sold for $5.448 million in 2018 to an unspecified buyer.

coverage (of which he doubtless would have approved), Telly Savalas, Ernest Borgnine, Robert Wagner, and Red Buttons.[230]

His passing was widely noted in the press, most of them referring to him as the Master of Disaster and none of them venturing beyond the perfunctory biography he had been recycling since the 1950s. *The Washington Post*, writing of him the next day, quoted a 1977 interview in which he said, "No, I'm not going to run out of disasters. Pick up the daily newspaper, which is my best source for crisis stories, and you'll find ten or fifteen every day."[231]

He was survived by his cousin, Al Gail, his widow, Sheila (who died on November 15, 2013), and a reputation that will live as long as the public buys tickets to see other people in danger.

---

230 Joseph McBride, *Variety*, November 4, 1991 and *The Hollywood Reporter*, November 7, 1991.

231 (unsigned) *The Washington Post*, November 3, 1991.

Chapter 16: A Final Observation

Getting a clear picture of Irwin Allen is like trying to put your finger on mercury, and *mercurial* is a word that describes him. He was a public figure who kept his private life a mystery, but whether he did so to hide something or merely to force others to focus on business can be debated but never solved. As flamboyant as any of Hollywood's legendary showmen—Cecil B. DeMille, Mike Todd, Joseph E. Levine, Dino DeLaurentiis, Otto Preminger, and even their lower-level pretenders—he became identified with a genre and was apparently satisfied to thrive within it.

What most people outside the industry never recognized was that Allen, who was always referred to as a producer, was also a prolific writer and director. Counting the episodes of his various television series, he can claim over three hundred credits as producer, seventeen as director, and at least twelve as writer, not including the stories he hired others to script and however many uncredited rewrites he did on his own. As we have seen, he wasn't a great writer or director, but he knew what he wanted and got it done, either by himself or someone else, within the constraints of time and budget.

In a town known for creating and tolerating egos, his was second to none. An "Irwin Allen Production" came to mean something. True, it was often a combination of showmanship, exploitation, puerility, and ambition, but it more often than not paid off at the box office. He made Hollywood films—professionally, consummately, and unashamedly. They may have been lowbrow but they were never condescending. Yet so sacred was the commercial notion of an "Irwin Allen Production" that his profile often obscured the efforts of others. There's no indication that he was a credit-grabber, but others seemed to regard it as their duty to do it on his behalf. The week after he died, for example, the *Los Angeles Times* ran a tiny correction noting that, "in his obituary on November 3, producer Irwin Allen was credited with being the director of the disaster epics *Towering Inferno* and *Poseidon Adventure*. The Directors Guild reports that John Guillermin was the principal unit director on *Towering Inferno* while Ronald Neame was principal director of *The Poseidon Adventure*. Allen, who produced both films, also directed the action sequences in each film."[232] Even in death, Irwin Allen stole the spotlight and it wasn't even his fault.

Why, then, no love, or such conditional love, for Irwin Allen?

As a hyphenate (writer-producer-director), Allen could claim he was as much of an auteur as, say, Billy Wilder, Blake Edwards, Stanley Kubrick, Christopher Nolan, Sergio Leone, or Quentin Tarantino, all of whom similarly wrote, directed, and produced their films. If that's all it takes, he was qualified. As pantheons go, this technically places him above John Ford, Howard Hawks, Frank Capra, Alfred Hitchcock, and George Cukor, every one of them a certified and celebrated auteur, but none of whom took writing credit on their films. Was it because Allen, like DeMille, produced popular entertainment and neither courted the critics nor reached for art? Was it because he labored in the realm of fantasy and science fiction, two genres that many critics still deem to be one step above comic books, which they also unfairly denigrate?

Allen made pictures for people, not critics. For profits, not awards. But also for fun, not as work. He had a hell of a time and wanted his audiences to have one, too.

Allen's other problem is that he peaked early. He won his Oscar® on March 19, 1953 for 1952's *The Sea Around Us*, a film he directed but on which he took no directing credit. He was thirty-seven. It was his first film in which he was completely in charge, and he succeeded right out of the chute, no more getting

---

232　"For the Record," *Los Angeles Times*, November 11, 1991.

pushed off of films he'd set up or denied credit by the studio. But it was just a documentary and he wanted to make "real" movies.

His films were not showy, they were show business. They were never pretentious, even though sometimes he was. His work is meat-and-potatoes, albeit prime rib, but never did they aspire to advance the art of cinema. He never directed a performer or writer to so much as an Academy Award® nomination, let alone a win, although some of his special effects collaborators took home technical Oscars. Even when *The Towering Inferno* was nominated for Best Picture in 1974, arguably because it had two studios' worth of voting Academy members putting it on the ballot, it lost to *The Godfather Part II* for reasons that need no explanation.

Allen himself was a workaholic but it paid off, so he loved it. Of the comments that everyone made about him, the phrases *very prepared* and *concerned for safety* always arise. He may have craved excess on the screen, but behind the screen he was conservative to the point of obsession.

Although he may have traveled with an entourage, he was a singular person who knew what was going on everywhere at all times.

He was, to all reports, a conventionally moral man. When there was romance to be had in his films and TV shows, it was chaste and perfunctory. In *The Towering Inferno*, even with two of the screen's most glamorous people—Faye Dunaway and Paul New-man—their single tryst is almost a parody of chaste movie love scenes. Had it not been for John Williams' music, one would not even know that the two of them were attracted to each other.

If Allen had a private life, he kept it that way. His name does not turn up in the gossip columns. As for legal matters, other than the Marineland debacle, the only intellectual property item was a gafuffa in 1960 when Gold Key published a comic book called *Space Family Robinson* that observers insisted influenced Allen when *Lost in Space* was being created (especially where the show's working title had been *Space Family Robinson*). But that was it; nothing came of it.[233]

For all intents and purposes, once Allen left the studio or went home from an awards dinner, he minded his own business. No tales of rampant starlets, drugs, or wall street shenanigans. Besides, he probably had four or five scripts to go over and fix, again without credit.

His legacy in film history is still open. His contribution to television is more assured: *Lost in Space* has had two reboots to date, *The Time Tunnel* has had one, and there are consistent rumors that *Voyage to the Bottom of the Sea* is set for a revival. *The Poseidon Adventure* was remade, and the only reason that *The Towering Inferno* hasn't been remade, rebooted, prequeled, or sequeled is that it is now controlled by Discovery and Disney (who bought Warners and Fox, respectively) and it would take an act of God to pull off an agreement between those two corporate behemoths. And even if anyone could, the true-life horrors of 9-11 would make any attempt to do so obscene beyond words.

In the end, Irwin Allen's greatest production was Irwin Allen. He was Hollywood all the way. Not the Hollywood that insiders know and some of them detest, but the Hollywood that outsiders dream about. He was good at giving people their fantasies because his life was a fantasy that he wrote, produced, directed, and, best of all, lived. *The Towering Inferno* turned out to be the pinnacle of that fantasy, and that's why it has survived.

---

233 https://cinemaretro.com/index.php?/archives/5631-LOST-IN-SPACE-THE-1960S-COMIC-BOOK-SCANDAL!.html

Afterword: Surviving Fire

Does The Towering Inferno accurately reflect fire danger in general in America or was it just another Hollywood fantasy, albeit one that was rooted in fact at the time it was made? A man who knows about both is Brian Cummings. Cummings was Chief of the Los Angeles Fire Department from 2011 to 2013, before which he was Assistant chief, and before that a firefighter. Among his objectives as Chief was to update the city's outdated technology. He supervised 3,500 LAFD employees. Since 2018 he has been technical consultant on the television series Station 19 through which he has gained perspective on the particular needs and limitations of entertainment in terms of the reality and responsibilities of fire safety. He was a kid when The Towering Inferno came out—his father was also a firefighter—and he deems the Irwin Allen movie remarkably accurate for the time it was made. Because his knowledge of fire and fire safety is so compelling, and the details so crucial, it is being presented in Q&A format edited only for continuity.

Nat Segaloff: 9-11 was a shocking example of how hard it is to escape from a high-rise building. Have we added any fire protection codes since then or there any advice you can give anyone who has to go above the third floor?

Brian Cummings: Absolutely. If you look at the history of fire codes in the United States it's the history of disasters in fires in America. Every major fire code change that we've had has stemmed out of a major fire where there have been civilian injuries or civilian loss of life. Improvements include ponet doors[234] inside buildings, sprinkler systems, automatic fire annunciator systems[235] in high-rise buildings, exhaust systems that are required in stairwells. Yes, there have been some changes that came out of 9-11, but the Trade Centers were already very, very safe buildings. They incorporated a lot of the most modern fire detection equipment, sealed stairwells, stairwell ventilation system. They were very, very robust and safe buildings. Some of the things that we got out of it were that we're looking more at evacuation and some of the homeland security issues. But were there actual fire code changes coming out of it? I'd have to say no, nothing really sparked off that which was required.

I was surprised to find that a lot of the building codes are designed to keep the building safe but they don't address the people inside them.

The fire service has worked quite hard to change that. One of the organizations is the NFPA (National Fire Protection Association) which brings together the builders, the unions, and the responders. The codes are designed to safely get people out of a building.to make sure that the building survives long enough so that there's a means of egress for everyone who's inside that building. What the fire codes don't address is that, while it may keep the building safe long enough to give them time to get out, they don't always address the safety of the firefighters that are working to suppress the fire and rescue occupants. We see that more often in lightweight residential construction where some of the lightweight roofing barely supports its own weight, so when you put a fire inside that building, impacting its structural integrity, when the firefighters get on those roofs, we see a lot of roof collapses. But nowadays the fire codes very much address the safety of the building occupants, whether it's regulating how

---

234 “Ponet Doors” *are doors that are required to be closed at all times at the junction of a hallway corridor and fire escape.*

235 A system that coordinates fire sensors and alarms.

many occupants in a building, how wide the access hallways are, how big stairwells are, how many stairwells are mandated from each floor, how many exits, how the exit lighting is done—so there's quite a bit done to get people safely out of that building should something go wrong.

Are combustible core panels still a problem?[236]

They are. We don't see that much in Los Angeles; in fact, you cannot have them in new construction as exterior decoration. The last time we had something here in L.A. was the MTA Transit Headquarters Tower near Union Station, a twenty-six story building that had decorative paneling around the top floor terrace. The paneling caught fire and It looked like we had a huge high-rise fire. It was an electrical short that caught that paneling on fire. But if you Google it, you'll see some buildings fires in Europe that are terrifying that go up basically like a torch.

Yes, there are some in Dubai. They go up like a Roman candle.

Following that fire in Los Angeles, the inspectors went out to the older buildings that potentially had that type of exterior paneling. But the Los Angeles fire code does not allow any kind of combustible exterior cladding on a building.

You've seen The Towering Inferno.

Oh yes. I saw it as a kid and have seen it several times since. I think every firefighter should see it. It's a really interesting example of how we fought high-rise fires back in the seventies.

How have things changed since then? A lot of local ordinances were changed as people became sensitized.

---

236   Decorative or structural covering that are sandwiches of polyurethane and aluminum. They are lightweight and can be bent to form curves but are dangerously unstable in case of fire.

Oh absolutely. There was also a large fire down in Sao Paolo that turned into a huge story. Yes, they looked into making sure that stairwells weren't going to be affected by an explosion, that they didn't have gas lines running through them, and they made sure that there was full ventilation in the stairwells and made them full smoke towers. [Inspectors] added more sprinkler systems, more fire hose systems inside, annunciator panels, automatic systems to shut off elevators so they didn't open up on fire floors if people took those elevators by mistake. Our latest in Los Angeles, the downtown Wilshire Grand, is an extremely safe building. They've actually got two banks of elevators that are built inside of a concrete elevator shaft that's supposed to withstand any kind of a fire that that building could get, so those elevators are actually safe to use in a fire. They've got multiple detection systems throughout every floor of that building so firefighters know exactly the nature of problem that they have and the quickest way to get to it. Things have really changed and been updated since *The Towering Inferno* debuted. High rise buildings have really improved; the safety factor has gone way up.

So does that mean that you would bring your family above the third floor?

Absolutely. For me it's the building rather than how high up you go. If I was going to be in an older high-rise building like the Biltmore [in L.A.] I'd ask for a lower floor because some of the systems are not as up to date as the newer buildings. But, when I travel, if I'm in a modern high-rise building, I'm comfortable going on any floor that they want to put me on, realizing that it could be a long hike down the stairwell if I need to get down.

How high can the average ladder truck reach?

In Los Angeles our aerials are a hundred feet long. Plazas and other decorative things keep the base of the ladder from getting close to the building which really restricts how high we can go. But if we have a building that's fronting right on a boulevard that we can get an aerial ladder close to, we can hit the seventh or eighth floor with that ladder, but more realistic is the fifth or sixth floor.

Stirling Silliphant said that he had lunch with a fire expert who insisted on a basement restaurant sitting under the sprinkler.

It's good to be cautious when you're in a building. I always tell people to know where two exits are. What most folks do in an emergency is head back the way they came in, and that may not be the closest or the best way to get out of a building. When I'm staying in a hotel on location, when I go down to a meal, I will ask people which way they turn out of their room door to get to the nearest stairwell, and it's amazing how many people don't stop to think about that. The time to think about it is before zero-dark-30 when there's smoke in the hallway and you're trying to remember which way the stairwell is. Knowing how to get out of a building, knowing where there's a firehose in the hallway, where the fire extinguisher is—having an idea of those things is really important to keeping you and your family safe.

One of the things I found stunning in the movie was when Steve McQueen asks the security guy about the businesses in the building and he says, "Oh, they're all out of here," and McQueen says, "you don't understand" and he goes into a litany of substances that create toxic fumes. Do people generally not think about what happens to their carpets and sofas?

Nobody thinks about it at all. If you think of the average living room, everything there, the furniture, the upholstery, the curtains, it's all materials made from petroleum. When petroleum burns it gives off toxic fumes and dense, black smoke. It burns extremely fast and, as it burns, it melts, and you get puddles of burning melted stuff on the ground. The NFPA has a demonstration video. They have two rooms side by side. One is a room with cotton drapery and wool upholstery, natural combustibles, and the second room has modern synthetic and polyesters. They tip over a candle on a sofa in both these rooms. In the room with the ordinary combustibles it's fifteen or twenty minutes before the entire room is engulfed in flames; it's about a minute and forty-five seconds before the modern room is engulfed in flames. It happens so fast. There's dripping, burning liquid on the ground. It spreads, and even the smoke from the burning synthetics is flammable and so toxic. In fact, toxicity is one of the biggest hazards in a modern high-rise fire.

What are the hazards in any fire? I understand that smoke is probably more deadly than flame.

Oh, absolutely, because smoke travels so widely throughout the structure. And smoke has an anesthetizing effect, which is why smoke detectors are so good because if you start gradually breathing in the smoke while you're asleep in bed, you'll stay asleep until you're dead. In the MGM Grand fire in 1980, eighty people died, all from smoke, just getting trapped, trying to find exits in hallways as the smoke filled the building. Smoke is the number one thing that kills people. Structural collapse is a tertiary cause behind smoke and fire. Buildings are engineered to be part of a whole, and as parts start to burn, you lose that integrity; you kick out one leg of a table, the table tips over. It's the same with houses. You burn out a certain number of joists or support beams, you start to get structural collapse. In modern construction in houses, we love open floor plans. You don't want doorways dividing you from spaces in your house. Tragically, the fire likes that as well because all those doors and individual compartments slow the fire and smoke down and buy you more time.

Is it better to crawl on your stomach to avoid the smoke or go on your hands and knees because the smoke settles?

In my experience fighting fires, being on all fours is better because you have more mobility, but I've been to fires where you're pressed down breathing right on the carpet. The smoke won't settle until it starts to cool. When the fire is still burning you get the stratification of all those heat layers, and two feet from the ground it's black and hot and smokey, but below two feet it's clear and you can see all the way across the room. We teach our rookies to get in and see as far as you can and get below the smoke layer and you can see where the flames are. Nowadays with our modern protective gear – you're wearing a self-contained breathing apparatus, you're wearing a Nomex hood,[237] you're carrying a thermal camera, you really don't experience as much of the heat fighting fires so firefighters tend to go into buildings more upright. You take a little bit more heat because you're not feeling it, but you can see through the smoke because you have a thermal imaging camera. But it extends our folks into more of a situation and then, if you have any equipment failure, it's farther to get out, and it puts firefighters into greater danger. So the technology is a curse as well as a blessing, although it has also saved many lives as well.

Let's talk about the movie end of what you do, namely that fire in a movie doesn't photograph the way fire in real life looks. How do you deal with that on Station 19?

That's very true. Looking at it from a new angle since working as a consultant on a TV series, I see the difficulties and the challenges of trying to film action inside a building that's burning. The very fact that fires are hot and smokey and you can't see inside a building, that doesn't make for good television. Trying to find that balance, no one's done it yet, they still struggle. I talk with the DPs (Director of Photography) and the camera operators all the time about how we bring that immersive experience to the audience that makes it as real as we possibly can while still showing the danger and the action that we want. It's

---

237 Nomex® is a brand of knit protective hood that covers head and shoulders.

a super hard challenge and, when they get it, it's going to have to be via imaging. You can't do it with [physical] special effects any more. There's no mechanical smoke that's dark enough for you or non-toxic enough for you, and flame bars are too regular. It's a combination of lighting effects and visual effects. If you don't have good lighting effects, visual effects won't do anything for you because it looks shallow. You see things happening but they don't light up the characters or the things around them. You need some mechanical smoke in there because it gives the VFX (visual effects) people something to paint on. (And you have to make sure you can see the actors' faces.) One of the biggest things is getting the actors not to wear their helmets down too low and to hold their chin up more so we can bounce the light on their face. It's definitely a problem actual firefighters don't have!

On The Towering Inferno *the fire effects people used propane. What do they use on* Station 19?

We use propane as well, but not very much. In the last season we use actual fire very rarely. If we're shooting outdoors we use flame bars here and there, either directly in front of the camera or hidden behind things to show that they were burning, but any time we were indoors, all season, it was visual effects. There are so many regulations now in order to be able to use propane and use live fire inside of a structure. The weather even weighs in on it; there are certain days of the year when you just can't burn even propane. So when you look at all the regulations and actors' safety and comfort for the camera crews and the sound people and the actors, visual effects probably works out to giving you the better bang for the buck. It looks more realistic and it allows the actors to do that acting stuff, and your lighting folk to be spot-on, too. Back in season three when we were using a lot more fire, after a few takes we'd have to turn on the ventilation and open the elephant doors and ventilate the heat and the smoke out of the set and there was a ten or fifteen minute delay between each take. The time adds up. We got really good acting because there was real fire there, but I don't think the fire scenes were that much better than the ones we did later using visual effects.

Do you ever use Zel-Jel, the heat-retarding gel invented by Gary Zeller?

The special effects guys use it on the stunt guys. Now you can get a lot closer, but those stunt performers are incredible people.

When a fireman burns himself, does he put butter on it?

No sir, we don't do butter. It's a wonderful old wives' tale. For any burn, cooling is the most important thing. If you have running water, run it until the pain goes away. Then put a dry dressing on it and go to your doctor. If the skin is broken you're going to be leaking bodily fluids anyway, and you don't want to put anything more that's wet on it. If it's a large area of skin, your body won't be able to regulate temperature and you can go into hypothermia. Infection is the biggest thing you're worried about.

The Towering Inferno shows people being blown though window glass. I thought high-rise windows were pretty solid. How do firefighters go about breaking them?

They're required by the fire codes that every few windows they have to have certain windows that are designed for firefighters to break out. It's got to be tempered glass so that it shatters into small pieces and falls off. There's a little mark down in the corner that lets us know that this is a window we can break. It's a little dot or a Maltese cross and you can just hit it with the tip of you axe or you can use a spring-loaded punch and the whole thing will just shatter and rain glass in tiny pieces like the side windshield does on your car.

Did you always want to be a fireman?

I didn't. My dad was a firefighter. My dad fought fires for the City of Los Angeles as a firefighter for thirty years. I went to UCLA as a freshman and I was going to be an electrical engineer following in my brother-law's footsteps. A year and a half into that I thought, "I don't want to sit at a desk my entire life." Seeing what my Dad had done his entire life in bringing us up and what he had done, I decided, when I was nineteen years old, that I wanted to be a firefighter. I got hired four days before my twenty-first birthday.

Much has changed over the years since you began.

This is opinion. I travel around the country speaking to groups and there are always older firefighters lamenting about the young guys "not having she skill set like we came up." And they're right; the firefighters we hire today have a totally different skill set that those we hired twenty years ago or the ones we hired forty years ago. But the job is changing and evolving as well, and we don't even know the skill set we will need. I need kids who are adept at social media and using a computer and Google searches, who are technically proficient, just as I need people from the construction trade or who have mechanical aptitude. I need people who have good bedside manner. Eighty-five percent of what a fire department does these days is emergency medical service. I need people who can hold somebody's hand in their darkest moment and make things just a little bit better. Because that's what they're paying us to do: show up when things are bad and make stuff a little bit better.

I never understood why they dispatch a fire truck along with an ambulance when it's just a stubbed toe.

We have to do that because we have a tiered system in Los Angeles, as do most major cities, which means that, depending on how severe the call is, we rate them from A to D with D being the lowest acuity call and A being a seizure or stroke or something like that, and we dispatch accordingly. So a D-level call may get a basic life support ambulance. A C-level call may get a paramedic ambulance by itself. When we get to a B-level call we know that it's going to take more than two paramedics to handle the problem that's there, so we send the two paramedics on an ambulance, but then we send the closest fire company as well because then we get four to six more extremely trained firefighter/EMTs that can help with things like carrying a patient, carrying equipment, setting drugs for the paramedics, doing all the things that we need to do. That's why we send the extra vehicles.

That's a question we frequently get asked by people: "He's having trouble breathing, why did an aerial ladder, an engine, and a rescue van show up?" Well, we know it's going to take more than two paramedics, and the way we get that additional staffing is on the fire engines. But then people ask–and a fire commissioner asked me this once–"Well why can't you just send another ambulance or send a pickup truck there?" I say, "that's an excellent idea, but what happens if, as soon as they clear that medical call, they get a fire call? Now they have to drive back to the station, get their gear, and then drive out to the fire." So just like when we're going to the supermarket or on a fire inspection, we take all our gear because we're on call 24/7 so we can respond to that call as soon as it comes in.

As technical advisor to a television show that doesn't want to run over budget, can you actually step in and stop them doing something that may b inaccurate?

(Laughs) I have learned, I have had this wonderful graduate education in the last four years. There's a triangle of things: there's reality, which is my spot; there's creative, what's the idea, what's the drama, what's the writer's vision; and then there's cost. All of those things are constantly battling. If I can give them a degree of reality that gives them their drama and is not too expensive, then we'll do it. But if it starts getting more expensive, and we have to compromise, the first thing we compromise is reality. I try to think of how I can get it "fire department-ish." And one of the things I've learned is that by choosing the right camera angles, they can make it look like it's something different. My first year we had a high-rise fire and I said we'd probably have forty or fifty fire engines, and we certainly couldn't get forty or fifty fire engines, so they used six, and it was brilliant because of the way they did it. They'd shoot one way and flip it around and put other numbers on it and shoot the other way. Even the background action: what would firefighters be doing logically in the fire? I don't need that, all we need to see is motion.[238] I started thinking of little things now and then, and I think it increased my value to them.

Have you ever been given any lines?

Season three they had me in one scene, a fire at a bowling alley. I was battalion chief that was the officer in command. I had a couple lines on camera and then four or five lines off camera. It was my big moment.

And you got your SAG card (Screen Actors Guild)

I certainly did! This year I think I'll poke 'em again. It's my fifth season, I want another role!

---

238 The company also hires many off-duty firefighters as extras, even giving some of them lines now and then.

Bibliography

American Cinematographer, Volume 56, Number 2, February, 1975; California: American Society of Cinematographers.

Bond, Jeff, *The Fantasy Worlds of Irwin Allen*, Sierra Madre, California: Creature Features, 2019.

Brownlow, Kevin, *The Parade's Gone By*, New York: Alfred A. Knopf, 1968.

Cushman, Marc and Mark Alfred, Foreword by Mark Phillips, *Irwin Allen's Voyage to the Bottom of the Sea, Volume One*, Los Angeles and Frazier Park, California: Jacobs/Brown Press, 2018.

Glut, Donald F., *The Dinosaur Scrapbook*, Secaucus, N.J.: Citadel, 1980.

Griffith, Richard and Arthur Mayer, with the assistance of Eileen Bowser, *The Movies*, Revised Edition, New York: Simon and Schuster, 1970.

Hilliard, Robert L., *The Broadcast Century: A Biography of American Broadcasting*, Stoneham, Massachusetts: Butterworth-Heinemann, 1992.

McGilligan, Patrick, editor, *Backstory 3*, California: University of California Press, 1997.

Scortia, Thomas N. and Frank M. Robinson, *The Glass Inferno*, New York: Pocket Books, 1974

Segaloff, Nat, "Stirling Silliphant: The Finger of God,"*Backstory 3*, Patrick McGilligan, ed., California: University of California Press, 1997; copyright transferred 2001; expanded into *Stirling Silliphant: The Fingers of God*, Albany, Georgia: BearManor Media, 2013.

Segaloff, Nat, *A Lit Fuse: The Provocative Life of Harlan Ellison*, Newton, Massachusetts: NESFA Press, 2017

Steinberg, Cobbett, *Reel Facts: The Movie Book of Records*, updated edition, New York: Vintage Books, 1982.

Stern, Richard Martin, *The Tower*, New York: Warner Paperback, 1973

Trager, James, *The People's Chronology*, First Revised Edition, New York: Henry Holt and Company, 1992.

Index

9 798888 771060 0